THE PEOPLE OF THE
WINDWARD ISLANDS
Trinidad and Tobago, and Curacao

1620 - 1860

By
David Dobson

CLEARFIELD

Printed for Clearfield Company by
Genealogical Publishing Company
Baltimore, Maryland
2019

ISBN 9780806358857

THE PEOPLE OF THE WINDWARD ISLANDS, TRINIDAD AND TOBAGO, AND CURACAO, 1620-1800

INTRODUCTION

The Windward Islands form part of the Lesser Antilles which stretch from Puerto Rico to the fringes of Venezuela. Since the seventeenth century these islands attracted immigrants from Europe, initially from Spain but soon also from the British Isles, France, the Netherlands, and Scandinavia. The Windward Islands comprise of Guadaloupe, Martinique, St Lucia, St Vincent, the Grenadines, Carriacou, Dominica, and Grenada.This volume also covers Curacao, Trinidad and Tobago, which lie close to the coast of Venezuela..

Though many of the early settlers arrived as economic migrants there were many that were transported as prisoners of war or escaping from persecution such as the Jews and the Huguenots. The contemporary economy and society of the West Indies was very much dependent on slaves brought from Africa. In due course some of the descendants of both ethnic groups chose to move to North America or to Europe.

This book is based on research into manuscript and published sources, mainly located in Great Britain, but also in the West Indies.

David Dobson,

Dundee, Scotland, 2018.

THE PEOPLE OF THE WINDWARD ISLANDS, TRINIDAD AND TOBAGO, AND CURACAO, 1620-1860

ABBOT, S. H. F., a barrister in Tobago, 1850s.

ADAIR, JOHN, in Grenada, 1777. [NLS.8793]

ADAMS, JOHN, aboard the John, commander Edward Clements, died in St Lucia ['St Lezee'] in the West Indies, probate, 1677, PCC. [TNA]

ADAM, HENRY, son of Robert Adam of Springbank, Falkirk, died in Grenada on 29 October 1861. [SGS.Lib]

ADAM. ROBERT, a Jacobite prisoner banished to the Leeward Islands, liberated by a French privateer and landed in Martinique in 1747. [TNA.SP36.102]

ADDIS, CHARLES, jr., a barrister of Lincoln's Inn, died in St Vincent on 2 December 1845. [GM.ns25.222]

ADYE, ABRAHAM CHARLES, the Attorney General, died in Grenada on 4 May 1815. [GM.85.646]

AFFLECK, DUNCAN, a staff surgeon, died in St Vincent on 7 March 1853. [EEC.22415]

AGARD, GEORGE, born 1831 in Barbados, settled in Tobago in 1850, a planter and merchant, died 1886.

AGERD, EDWARD, a soldier from London, in the service of the Dutch West India Company in Curacao before 1642. [GAR.ONA.95.178-289]

AGNEW, JAMES, Clerk of the Crown in Dominica in 1847. [DC27.2.1847]

AGNEW, WILLIAM, only brother of Nathaniel Agnes of Ochiltree, died in Mornsendue, Grenada, on 7 February 1779. [SM.41.286]

AGNEW, WILLIAM JAMES, son of Dr Agnew in Bristol, died in Dominica on 23 October 1848. [GM.ns31.222]

THE PEOPLE OF THE WINDWARD ISLANDS, TRINIDAD AND TOBAGO, AND CURACAO, 1620-1860

AIKEN, THOMAS, in Dominica, probate, 1802, PCC. [TNA]

AINSLIE, CHARLES DOUGLAS, youngest son of Thomas Ainslie of Wells, died in Grenada in January 1803. [EA.4105.03][AJ.2686]

AINSLIE, JAMES, a merchant in Grenada, was admitted as a burgess of Montrose, Angus, in 1771. [MBR]

AIRD, JOHN MACKENZIE, in Grenada, heir to his father Alexander Aird, a merchant in Invergordon, 13 March 1850, and to his uncle George Mackenzie in Culcragie, Scotland, 19 February 1856, also to his cousin Margaret Mackenzie in Invergordon, 19 February 1856, also to his grand-uncle George Mackenzie in Invergordon, on 20 February 1860. [NRS.S/H]; MCP, married Annette, widow of John Cameron, in Tempe House, Grenada, on 11 June 1863. [S.2521]

AITCHISON, DAVID, son of David Aitchison and his wife Elspeth Fairbairn in Highlaw, Coldingham, Berwickshire, died in Tobago in 1827. [Coldingham Priory gravestone]

AITCHISON, JOHN, from Airdrie, died in Grenada on 31 May 1780. [Glasgow Mercury.iii.286]

ALBONY, JOHN B., from Martinique, applied for citizenship in a Federal Court in South Carolina on 20 September 1797. [SCA]

ALBURN, ROBERT, in Dominica, probate, 1809, PCC. [TNA]

ALEXANDER, ALEXANDER JOHN, in Grenada, probate, 1801, PCC. [TNA]

ALEXANDER, or LLOYD, CHRISTINA, in St Lucia, heir to Marie Jean Alexander in St Lucia, 22 February 1839; widow of Ebenezer Lloyd a merchant in London, heir to her sister Robertina Alexander in St Lucia who died on 14 January 1866, 14 February 1867. [NRS.S/H]

THE PEOPLE OF THE WINDWARD ISLANDS, TRINIDAD AND TOBAGO, AND CURACAO, 1620-1860

ALEXANDER, ISABEL, in Grenada, a testament, 1869. [NRS.SC70.I.145/561]

ALEXANDER, JEANETTE MARY, in St Lucia, heir to her sister Robertina Alexander in St Lucia who died on 14 January 1866, 14 February 1867. [NRS.S/H]

ALEXANDER, JOHN, born 1800 in Banffshire, died 27 March 1840 on Morne Fendue Estate, Grenada. [AJ.4823]

ALEXANDER, JOHN, born 1801, third son of Charles Alexander a merchant in Glasgow, died in St George, St Vincent, on 12 September 1821. [SM.90.138]

ALEXANDER, MARY, wife of J. J. Alexander n St Lucia, and widow of Robert Cullen, Lord of Session and the Judiciary in Scotland, died in St Lucia on 10 February 1818. [GM.88.569]

ALEXANDER, ROBERTINA, heir to Marie Jean Alexander in St Lucia, 22 February 1839. [NRS.S/H]

ALEXANDER, THEODORE, a merchant in Grenada, 1772. [NRS.RGS.112.131; RS27.200.286]

ALEXANDER, WILLIAM, a merchant in St Lucia, owner of the Experiment of Glasgow, 1794. [NRS.CE60.11.4/86]

ALEXANDER, WILLIAM, from St Vincent, died in London on 18 January 1814. [GM.84.299]

ALEXANDER, WILLIAM, sometime in St Lucia, a sasine, 1825. [NRS.RS54.2734/4210]

ALLAN, MATTHEW, a cabinet maker in Grenada, 1834. [NRS.CS46.1834.7.71]

ALLAN, CHARLES, from Bristol, died in Dominica in 1795. [GM.65.794]

3

THE PEOPLE OF THE WINDWARD ISLANDS, TRINIDAD AND TOBAGO, AND CURACAO, 1620-1860

ALLEN, J. A., the Colonial Treasurer, married Sarah Leach, daughter of Hugh Leach in Bristol, in Port of Spain, Trinidad, on 15 June 1843. [GM.ns20.312]

ALLAN, WILLIAM, a merchant in Paisley, heir to his cousin George Allan in Grenada, 26 December 1834. [NRS.S/H]

ALLARDYCE, JAMES, in St Vincent, married Susanna Keith, daughter of James Keith, Excise Collector in Dundee, there on 1 November 1796. [SM.58.791]

ALLEYNE, ..., son of Bouverie Alleyne the Colonial Secretary, was born in St Vincent on 14 January 1861, [GM.ns2/10.453]

ALLPORT, RICHARD, a merchant from Bristol, died in Trinidad on 26 July 1829. [GM.99.286]

ALVES, WILLIAM GEMMILL, from St Vincent, formerly a Captain of the 29th Regiment, died in Brighton on 22 April 1860. [GM.ns2/8.641]

ANDERSON, ALEXANDER, born 1748, educated at Edinburgh University, to New York in 1774, in Surinam during the American Revolution but captured by a privateer and landed on Martinique, settled in St Lucia, later a botanist in St Vincent, died 1811.

ANDERSON, DAVID, only son of David Anderson a merchant in Dundee, died in Curacao on 30 November 1807, on arrival from Monte Video. [SM.70.317]

ANDERSON, HENRY H., a solicitor and notary public in Port of Spain, Trinidad, 1846. [TS:1.1.1846]

ANDERSON, JAMES, a Jacobite prisoner banished to the Leeward Islands, liberated by a French privateer and landed in Martinique in 1747. [TNA.SP36.102]

ANDERSON, Dr JAMES, a Fellow of the Royal College of Surgeons of Edinburgh, died in Port of Spain, Trinidad, on 30 September 1826. [BM.21.119]; a deed of attorney, Trinidad, 4 March 1815. [NRS.RD5.73.29]

ANDERSON, JOHN, a Jacobite prisoner banished to the Leeward Islands, liberated by a French privateer and landed in Martinique in 1747. [TNA.SP36.102]

ANDERSON, THOMAS, MD in Trinidad, heir to his father James Anderson a surgeon in Antigua, 20 October 1829. [NRS.S/H]

ANDERSON, WILLIAM, in Dominica, eldest son and heir of William Anderson a merchant in London, deeds, 1821. [NRS.RD5.215.579; RD5.213.521]; heir to his aunt Rachel Anderson daughter of Henry Anderson a farmer in Broughton, Edinburgh, also heir to his aunt Jean Anderson or Sommers, wife of William Sommers an innkeeper in Edinburgh, and heir to his aunt Margaret Anderson or Bogue, wife of John Bogue in Edinburgh, also heir to his uncle Henry Anderson, son of Henry Anderson a farmer in Broughton, 1822/1824. [NRS.S/H]

ANDERSON, Dr, Superintendent of the Botanical Gardens, died in St Vincent on 7 September 1811. [SM.74.155]

ANDERSON, ..., from Inverness, a magistrate in Kingston, St Vincent, in 1838. [AJ.4719]

ANSTRUTHER, CHARLES, son of Sir Philip Anstruther of Balcaskie, died in Dominica on 26 January 1778. [Ruddiman's Weekly Mercury.22]

ARCHIBALD, CHARLES, son of S. G. Archibald, 22 Windsor Street, Edinburgh, died on Plaisance Estate, Trinidad, on 12 May 1869. [S.8073]

THE PEOPLE OF THE WINDWARD ISLANDS, TRINIDAD AND TOBAGO, AND CURACAO, 1620-1860

ARMOUR, ROBERT, a surgeon in Trinidad, heir to his brother Hugh Armour a skipper in Irvine, 1 May 1823. [NRS.S/H]; married Ann Palmer, daughter of Mr Palmer a merchant planter in Trinidad, at Cauva, Trinidad on 29 September 1822. [DPCA.1074]

ARMSTRONG, GEORGE, son of Archibald Armstrong a gentleman in Grenada, matriculated at Glasgow University in 1808. [MAGU.238]

ARMSTRONG, WILLIAM, son of W. Armstrong a merchant in Glasgow, died in St Vincent on 22 September 1800. [GM.70.1214]

ARNAULT, THOMAS CHABAUD, in Dominica in 1772. [JCTP.1772.319]

ARNOLD, WILLIAM, from Grenada, died in London on 8 April 1807, [GM.77.489]; probate, 1807, PCC. [TNA]

ARNOLD, WILLIAM FITCH, married Elizabeth Cecilia Ruddach, only daughter of Alexander Ruddach, in Tobago, on 19 May 1819. [GM.88.480]

ARRINDELL, ELIZA, daughter of Isaac Arrindell, married John Primrose, son of Reverend Primrose in Prestonpans, in St Vincent on 2 May 1829. [BM.26.257]

ASHTON, HENRY, a merchant in Dominica in 1840. [DC:1.8.1840]

ASHWELL, CHARLES, in Grenada, married Fanny Whitehouse, youngest daughter of Edward Whitehouse, in Surrey, on 18 August 1792. [GM.62.766]

ATKINSON, WILLIAM, husband of Ruth, planters in Antigua later in Dominica, parents of George, born 1767, died 5 December 1779, and William [died 1782]. [St John's monument]

ATTWELL, ELIZABETH, born in Nevis, a widow, married Robert Thomas from Elie, Fife, in Curacao on 7 March 1719. [Extract uit het Trouwboek der Gereformeerde Gemente op het eiland Curacao van der jaar 1714 tot en met 1722]

ATTWOOD, THOMAS, former Chief Judge of Dominica, died in the King's Bench prison on 27 June 1793. [GM.63.676]

AUCHTERLONIE, ALEXANDER, settled in Dominica by 1765. [NRS.GD126, Box 4]

AUFFRAY, CLAUDE, senior, in Dominica in 1771. [JCTP.1773.274]

AUFFRAY, CLAUDE, junior, in Dominica in 1771. [JCTP.1773.274]

AUFFREY, FRANCOIS, in Dominica in 1771. [JCTP.1773.274]

AUCHTERSON, JAMES, Special Chief Justice, died in Castries, St Lucia, on 21 November 1838. [SG.8/738]

AULD, ROBERT, in Tobago, testament, 1864. [NRS.CS70.1.10/809]

AYTON, A., born 1772, from Lynn, died in St Vincent on 2 July 1801. [GM.71.859]

BACKERUS, JOANNIS, a Dutch Reformed Church pastor on Curacao in 1640s. [SAA.ACA.379/224]

BACKHOUSE, WILLIAM, only son of William Backhouse in Sedburgh, Yorkshire, died in Trinidad on 24 May 1800. [GM.70.901]

BAGNELL, EDWARD, a merchant late of St Pierre, Martinique, then in Trinidad, a deed, 5 Aril 1817. [NRS.RD5.115.444]

BAILLIE, ALEXANDER, of Dochfour, in Grenada, 1800. [NRS.GD23.6.477]; in Grenada, probate, 1802, PCC. [TNA]

BAILLIE, DAVID, a planter at Auchensheoch Estate, Tobago, 1836. [TNA.T71.1572]

THE PEOPLE OF THE WINDWARD ISLANDS, TRINIDAD AND TOBAGO, AND CURACAO, 1620-1860

BAILLIE, EVAN, born 1747, a merchant, emigrated via Plymouth aboard the Albion bound for St Vincent in January 1775, [TNA.T47.9/11]; in St Vincent, a sasine, 1776. [NRS.RGS.116.101]

BAILLIE, G., a former merchant in St Vincent, died in Brighton on 28 July 1809. [GM.79.785]

BAILLIE, JAMES, a merchant in Grenada, married Katherine Gordon, daughter of Robert Gordon of Hallhead, in Edinburgh on 14 February 1784. [Edinburgh Marriage Register]

BAILEY, MICHAEL, died in St George, Grenada, on 16 March 1847. [AJ.5182]

BAIN, GEORGE, a Jacobite prisoner banished to the Leeward Islands, liberated by a French privateer and landed in Martinique in 1747. [TNA.SP36.102]

BAIRD, JOHN, on Plantation Montreuil, parish of St Patrick, Grenada, 1792. [NRS.GD237.12.52]

BALFOUR, JOHN, in Tobago, 1772, [NRS.RD2.244/1.409]; eldest son of John Balfour Crawford of Powmiln and his wife Elizabeth Maxwell, a deed of attorney, Burleigh Castle, Tobago, 18 August 1778, [NRS.RD4.775.176]; 1790, [NLS.ms5028.40]; an executor in 1810. [NRS.RD3.336.135]

BALFOUR, Mrs, wife of Lieutenant Colonel William Balfour of the 57th Regiment, died in Trinidad on 6 July 1802. [GM.72.878]

BALLANTYNE, JAMES, a merchant from Edinburgh, then in St Vincent, 1802. [NRS.AC7.75]

BALLENY, THOMAS, from Trinidad, died in Edinburgh on 13 June 1832. [EEC.18876]

BANKS, A, a dispensing chemist in Trinidad in 1843. [PSG.1806]

THE PEOPLE OF THE WINDWARD ISLANDS, TRINIDAD AND TOBAGO, AND CURACAO, 1620-1860

BANNATYNE, JAMES, son of .... Bannatyne in St Calmer, Bute, died in St Vincent in 1806. [DPCA.209][AJ.3055]

BAPTIST, JEAN, in Dominica in 1771. [JCTP.1773.248]

BARBER, JOSEPH, born 1833, son of Thomas Barber and his wife Madelina McLeod, died in Trinidad on 10 October 1865. [Bellie gravestone, Banffshire]

BARBOUR, JOHN, a merchant from Glasgow, in St Vincent, 1834. [NRS.SC58.59.14.89]

BARCLAY, ANN, in Carriacou near Grenada in 1801, see John Barclay's will.

BARCLAY, JOHN, late of Carriacou near Grenada, in Cupar, Fife, son of Catherine Melville or Simpson in Cupar, a will, 1801. [NRS.SC20.33.14]

BARNETT, HARRY FREDERICK, born 1815, a surgeon, youngest son of Dr Barnett in Worcester, died in Trinidad on 30 December 1853. [GM.ns41.439]

BARRELL, THEODORE, a merchant in Grenada, a Loyalist Claim, 1783. [TNA.AO.13.137.4]

BARRY, DAVID, in Grenada, probate, 1809, PCC. [TNA]

BARTLETT, PATRICK, from Banff, then in Carriacou, the Grenadines, and later in London, the executor of Joseph Cumming, 1799. [NRS.CC8.8.131]

BASANTA, FERDINAND, King Street, Kingstown, St Vincent, 1870. [SVW:11.8.1870]

BASDEN, ROBERT HOME, born 1799, died in Dominica on 21 November 1852. [GM.ns39.216]

BAYNES, SARAH ANNE, wife of Edwin Baynes, died in Grenada on 4 September 1866. [GM.ns3/2.695]

BEARE, JAMES, from Topsham, Devon, died in Grenada on 4 January 1842. [GM.ns18.223]

BEATON, WILLIAM, born in Langside, Aberdeenshire, graduated from King's College, Aberdeen, minister of St Patrick's in Grenada from 1851 until 1856, died in Aberdeen in 1857. [F.7.667][KCA.291]

BEATSON, JAMES, eldest son of Henry Beatson, Commander of the Princess Elizabeth, died in Trinidad on 13 March 1807. [SM.69.477]

BEATTY, WILLIAM, in Grenada, probate 1776, PCC. [TNA]

BEAUPIERRE, JOHN, constable in St Patrick's, Trinidad, 1847. [DC.27.2.1847]

BECK, ARBRAHAM, Governor of Curacao from 1708 to 1710

BECK, JACOB, Governor of Curacao from 1704 to 1708. [NWIC.201-163]

BECK, MATTHIAS, Vice Governor of Curacao from 1655 to 1664.

BEDWATER, DAVID, constable in St Patrick's, Dominica, 1847. [DC:27.2.1847]

BEECH, THOMAS, a surgeon from Bracknell, Berkshire, died in Dominica in October 1812. [GM.83.284]

BEEKS, WILLEM, Governor of Curacao in 1670. [PCCol.1670.906]

BEESLY, WILLIAM LUCAS, in Tobago, probate, 1801, PCC. [TNA]

BELL, ALINE, youngest daughter of Thomas Bell, from Stockton on Tees, the President of Dominica, married John Richard Walcot, on Black Bay Estate, Grenada, on 15 December 1859. [GM.ns2/8.289]

BELL, GEORGE, born 1795, son of Robert Bell and his wife Jane Hamilton in Netherbyres Mill, Ayton, Berwickshire, died in Tobago on 17 February 1822, [Ayton gravestone]

BELL, THOMAS, of the Commissary's Department, son of T. Bell in London, died in Trinidad on 6 May 1817. [GM.87.638]

BELL, THOMAS, born 1800, President of Dominica, died there on 14 October 1861. [GM.ns2/11.692]

BELL, WILLEM, a resident of Curacao in 1735. [Brieven en Papieren van Curacao.]

BELL, WILLIAM, born 1700, a book-seller in Berwickshire, a Jacobite banished to the Leeward Islands, liberated by a French privateer and landed on Martinique in 1747. [P.2.32][TNA.SP36.102]

BELLAIR, CHARLES MARTIN ROGER, in Dominica in 1775-1776. [JCTP.1775.441; 1776.13]

BELLAIR, FRANCIS ROGER, in Dominica in 1770s, [JCTP.1772.319; 1775.441; 1776.13]; leased lands in Dominica in 1773. [JCTP.1773.80]

BELLAIR, MARTIN ROGER, leased lands in Dominica in 1773. [JCTP.1773.80]

BELLAIR, ROGER, in Dominica in 1772. [JCTP.1772.319]

BELLOT, GALVAN, warden of St Mark's parish, Dominica, in 1847. [DC27.2.1847]

BELLOT, BENOIT, warden of St Paul's parish, Dominica, in 1847. [DC27.2.1847]

BELLAT, LEWIS F., a merchant in Dominica, 1840. [DC:1.8.1840]

THE PEOPLE OF THE WINDWARD ISLANDS, TRINIDAD AND TOBAGO, AND CURACAO, 1620-1860

BELTRAN CANCEDA Y VALESCO, AGUSTIN, born in Bogota, an Augustinian priest, Apostolic Prefect of Curacao from 1734 until his death in 1738.

BENNETT, ALEXANDER, warden of St Andrew's parish, Dominica, in 1847. [DC27.2.1847]

BENNETT, EMMA, eldest daughter of Robert Ward in Brighton, wife of magistrate Charles Bennett, died in St Lucia on 19 October 1839. [GM.ns13.333]

BENNETT, WILLIAM, born 1754, a farmer from Worcester, emigrated via London aboard the <u>Britannia</u> bound for St Vincent in January 1774. [TNA.T47.9-11]

BERKELEY, MARY, widow of Thomas Berkeley in Grenada, married Major W. H. Hartman of the 9th Regiment, in London on 12 July 1842. [GM.ns18.312]

BERKELEY, S. H., Lieutenant Colonel of the 16th Regiment, Deputy Adjutant of the Windward and Leeward Islands, married Elizabeth Murray, second daughter of William Murray, in Barbados on 24 February 1818. [GM.88.464]

BERNAGIE, BASTIAAN, to Curacao as an employee of the Dutch New West India Company around 1682, Governor there from 1692 to his death in 1700. [NWIC.I.88/106]

BERNOE, ..., a gentleman in Curacao in 1709. [SPAWI.1709.411]

BERTRAND, E. R., in Tabery, Dominica, married Frances Elizabeth Newton, daughter of R. Newton of Coldrey, Hampshire, in Froyle, Hampshire, on 1 February 1823. [GM.93.272]; she died in Dominica on 7 December 1842. [GM.ns19.556]

BETHUNE, Dr GEORGE, from Tobago, was admitted as a burgess of Banff in 1800. [Banff burgess roll]

BEUSE, CHARLES, in St Vincent in 1773. [JCTP.1773.334]

BEUSE, JEAN, in St Vincent in 1773. [JCTP.1773.334]

BEUSE, PHILIP, in St Vincent in 1773. [JCTP.1773.334]

BINCKES, JACOB, Dutch Governor of New Walcheren, [Tobago], built Fort Sterreschans in 1676, killed there by the French in December 1677. [PCCol.1678; 1211/1237]

BIRD, JAMES, born 1802, eldest son of John Bird and his wife Isabella Howden, a merchant in Kingstown, St Vincent, died there on 6 January 1844. [Chirnside gravestone, Berwickshire]

BIRD, JOHN, born 1745, a merchant in Bristol, from Bristol aboard the Neptune bound for Grenada in January 1774. [TNA.T47.9-11]

BIRNIE, JAMES, sometime a planter in Tobago, later in Techmuiry, testament, 1799, Comm. Aberdeen. [NRS]

BIRRELL, GEORGE, former Attorney General of St Lucia and the Bahamas, died in Nassau, New Providence, on 9 March 1837. [GM.ns7.670]

BLACKALL, Mrs, wife of Lieutenant Governor Blackall, died in Dominica on 2 May 1853. [GM.ns40.98]

BLACKWOOD, PERCY, born 1840, the Colonial Secretary of Tobago, youngest son of Sir Henry S. Blackwood, died in Southsea, Hampshire, on 1 June 1866. [GM.ns3/2.119]

BLAIR, JAMES, from Irvine, Ayrshire, died in St Vincent on 18 August 1818. [S.94.18]

BLENAC, Count, Governor of Martinique in 1686. [SPAWI.1730.324]

BLEAU, DIDER, constable in St Mark's, Dominica, 1847. [DC:27.2.1847]

THE PEOPLE OF THE WINDWARD ISLANDS, TRINIDAD AND TOBAGO, AND CURACAO, 1620-1860

BLONDEL, ..., in Martinique in 1724. [SPAWI.1724.400ii]

BLUCKE, R., fourth son of Reverend Robert Blucke in Edlesborough, Buckinghamshire, died in Tobago on 11 November 1833. [GM.104.343]

BOGLE, ROBERT, born 1724, via London to Grenada aboard the Ann Teresa in February 1774. [TNA.T47.9-11]

BOGLE, ROBERT, in Grenada, a deed, 31 March 1772. [NRS.RD2.224/2.650]

BOGLE, ROBERT, sr., a merchant in Grenada, died on 1 June 1777. [SM.39.455]

BOGLE, ROBERT, son of Michael Bogle a merchant in Glasgow, died in Tobago on 10 March 1791. [SM.53.258]

BOGLE, THOMAS, eldest son of Jacob Bogle a police lieutenant in Edinburgh, died in Trinidad in March 1818. [BM.3.630]

BOLAND, LOUIS, constable in St Mark's, Trinidad in 1847. [DC.17.2.1847]

BOLTON, Sir JOHN, in St Vincent, probate, 1807, PCC. [TNA]

BOMBRON, Captain, master of Le Modere at Martinique in 1702. [SPAWI.1702.195]

BONAMI, Madame, in St Vincent in 1767. [JCTP.1767.283]

BONTEEN, JAMES, an engineer in Dominica, son of Archibald Bonteen deceased, a deed, 1774. [NRS.RD4.216.299]

BONY, PETER, constable in St Patrick's, Dominica, 1847. [DC:27.2.1847]

BOONE, JOHN, in Dominica in 1772. [JCTP.79.8]

BOOTH, JAMES, in Martinique, later in Aberdeen, testament, 27 January 1812, Comm. Aberdeen. [NRS]

THE PEOPLE OF THE WINDWARD ISLANDS, TRINIDAD AND TOBAGO, AND CURACAO, 1620-1860

BOUDEWIJNS, LUDOVICUS, briefly Governor of Curacao, 1665.

BOUGOUD, ADOLPHE, Clerk of the Peace for the Naparima District of Trinidad, 1843. [PSG:1806]

BOWEN, J. TOWNSEND, from Trinidad, married Jessie Courthope, youngest daughter of T. Courthope in London, in Camberwell on 14 June 1838. [GM.ns10.207]

BOWIE, JOHN, born 1732, a servant in Aberdeen, a Jacobite banished to the Leeward Islands, liberated by the French and landed in Martinique in 1747. [P.2.44][TNA.SP36.102]

BOYCE, THOMAS, born 1759, a clerk in London, emigrated from London aboard the <u>Westerhall</u> bound for the Grenades in November 1774. [TNA.T47.9/11]

BOYER, JOSEPH, constable in St Andrew's, Dominica, 1847. [DC:27.2.1847]

BOYLE, WILLIAM, born in Penpont, Dumfries-shire, a partner in Boyle and Strickland in Trinidad, died in Liverpool in 1818. [EA.5742.23]

BRADFORD, HENRY J., Colonial Secretary of Dominica in 1840. [DC:1.8.1840]

BRANDER, Mr, in Grenada, was killed in a duel in St George, Grenada, on 16 April 1799. [GM.69.621]

BRANDER, JOHN, in Grenada, died on Tortula on 18 May 1806, [GM.76.776]; probate, 1807, PCC. [TNA]

BRASH, FRANCIS BANKS, born 1843, son of Alexander Brash, a sugar plantation manager in Trinidad, and his wife Agnes Denham, married Jane Graham McNee, born 1841, daughter of Duncan McNee and his wife Elizabeth Marshall, in Glasgow on 22 January 1867, died on Lothians Estate, Trinidad on 21 March 1892. [Glasgow, Anderston, 1861/28][Trinidad, Savannah Grande, 1892/486]

BRENNE, JOHN, in Dominica in 1771. [JCTP.78.186]

BRENNE, JOHN BAPTIST, in Dominica in 1771. [JCTP.78.186]

BRIDGEMAN, SOPHIA CATHARINE, wife of John Bridgman the Customs Collector of St Lucia, died there on 20 December 1812. [GM.83.181]

BRIDGEWATER, HENRY, from Grenada, married Isabella Shaw, daughter of James Shaw in Muirton, in Forres in 1813. [EA.5195.13]

BRIDGEWATER, SHAW, warden of St Andrew's parish, Dominica, in 1847. [DC27.2.1847]

BRISBANE, Sir CHARLES, born 1772, fourth son of Admiral Brisbane in Ayrshire, Governor and Captain General of St Vincent, died 11 January 1829. [St Vincent gravestone]

BRISBANE, THOMAS STEWART JAMES, third son of Sir C. Brisbane, Governor of St Vincent, died in 1812. [GM.82.493]

BROAD, CHARLES, former machinery superintendent of Drury Lane Theatre, died in St Vincent on 15 October 1837. [GM.ns7.447]

BRODIE, Reverend GEORGE, born 1815, a missionary of the United Presbyterian Church, died 7 October 1875 in Port of Spain, Trinidad. [EC.28419]

BROUSSE, GABRIEL, in Dominica in 1772. [JCTP.1773.280]

BROUWERS, THEODORUS, a Franciscan priest and Apostolic Prefect on Curacao in 1776

BROWN, Major ALEXANDER, Deputy Governor of Tobago, was served heir to his father Thomas Brown in Huntly on 4 July 1766. [NRS.S/H]; Governor of Tobago, died 1766. [GM.36.405]

BROWN, BENJAMIN, born 1796, a hospital assistant, died in Grenada in 1817. [S.32.17]

16

BROWN, CHARLES, youngest son of John Osburn Brown a Writer to the Signet, died in Grenada on 30 January 1820. [BM.7.231]

BROWN, DUNCAN, a merchant in Kingston, St George's, St Vincent, 1822. [NRS.AC7.100.1019]

BROWN, EDWARD, son of John Brown a merchant in Glasgow, died in Grenada on 18 July 1796. [GM.66.880]

BROWNE, ELIZABETH, born 1785, second daughter of John Browne in Grenada, died in Reigate on 23 March 1858. [GM.ns2/4.566]

BROWN, FRANCIS, from Trinidad, married Elizabeth Smith, daughter of John Smith a bookseller, in Glasgow on 11 October 1822. [BM.12.691]; their daughter was born on Jordanhill Estate, Trinidad, on 2 March 1824, [F.114]; he died on 15 January 1826 in Jordanhill Estate, Trinidad. [BM.19.765]

BROWN, FRANCIS, died at Belaire, St Vincent on 8 September 1829. [BM.27.134]

BROWN, H., died on passage from Grenada to England on 25 July 1803. [GM.73.987]

BROWN, JAMES, a physician and surgeon, ADC to the Earl of Huntingdon, died in Dominica on 26 January 1824. [S.447.256]

BROWN, JAMES WILLIAM, born 1793, a Counsellor of St Vincent, died in London on 2 February 1847. [St Vincent gravestone] [GM.ns27.328]

BROWN, JOHN, from Elgin, a surveyor in Tobago in 1780. [NLS.ms2385/2-7]; a carpenter of Harmony Hall, Tobago, testament, 31 December 1808, Comm. Aberdeen. [NRS]

BROWN, JOHN, a mariner in Kingston, St Vincent, later a skipper in Greenock in 1822. [NRS.AC7.100.1019]

BROWN, JOHN, from Glasgow, died in Bellaire, St Vincent, on 29 October 1828. [BM.25.682]

BROWN, JOSEPH, a Jacobite banished to the Leeward Islands, liberated by the French and landed on Martinique n 1747. [P.2.54][TNA.SP36.102]

BROWN, JOSIAS, from Glasgow, a Wesleyan missionary in St Vincent, married Martha Amelia, youngest daughter of Captain J. Keens from Bristol, in Tobago on 4 January 1842. [GSP.707]

BROWN, ROBERT, born 1762 in Springtown, Ireland, an Assemblyman of St Vincent, died on 20 October 1830. [St Vincent gravestone]

BROWN, ROBERT, born 1742, a watchmaker from London, emigrated via London aboard the Squirrel bound for the Grenades in December 1773. [TNA.T47.9-11]

BROWN, SUSAN HARRIET, only daughter of Colonel Thomas Brown, married Allan McDowell, MD, in St Vincent on 4 July 1818. [GM.88.273][BM.3.117]

BROWN, THOMAS, born 1760, died in St George, Grenada, on 30 September 1846. [GM.ns27.110]

BROWN, WILLIAM, a merchant in St Kitts, later a planter of Lower Quarter Plantation, St David's parish, Tobago, died 1767, a deed. [NRS.B10.15.7493]

BROWNHILLS, THOMAS, born 1725, a labourer in Inchture, a Jacobite banished to the Leeward Islands, liberated by the French and landed on Martinique n 1747. [P.2.54][TNA.SP36.102]

BROWNLEE, ALEXANDER, born 1726, a watchmaker in Edinburgh, a Jacobite banished to the Leeward Islands, liberated by the French and landed on Martinique in 1747. [P.2.54][TNA.SP36.102]

BRUCE, ALEXANDER, born 1818, son of William Bruce in Langholm, died 1851 in St Vincent. [Dundonald gravestone]

BRUCE, ANDREW, son of David Bruce of Kinnaird, died in St Vincent on 25 August 1773. [SM.35.616]

BRUCE, GEORGE, Captain of HM Engineers, with his wife, aboard the Greyhound at Plymouth bound for Dominica in December 1773. [TNA.T47.9/11]

BRUCE, JAMES, in Dominica, see deed dated 1 January 1785. [NRS.RD2.242.1.103]; a merchant in Dominica, son of Captain James Bruce of the 26th Regiment, 18 August 1791. [NRS.SC20.36.15]

BRUCE, JAMES, in Martinique, probate 1797, PCC. [TNA]

BRUCE, JAMES, Lieutenant Governor of Dominica, married Margaret Thomson, daughter of John Thomson of Spring Gardens on 30 November 1798. [SM.60.864]. She, his widow, died there in 1817, testament, 1818, Comm. Edinburgh. [NRS]; he died in London on 22 April 1808, [GM.78.464]; James Bruce, in Dominica, probate, 1808, PCC. [TNA]

BRUCE, JAMES, from St Vincent, died in Bath on 14 April 1815. [GM.85.473]

BRUCE, JOHN, a merchant in Grenada, son of John Bruce of Tulligarth, the Sheriff Substitute of Clackmannan, deeds, 1819, [NRS.RD5.157.493; 159.216]; later in Edinburgh in 1821. [NRS.CS17.1.40/271]

BRUCE, JOHN, in Dominica, later in Sierra Leone, an indenture re Sugar Loaf Plantation, St John's parish, Dominica, 9 July 1823. [Caribbeana.3.309]

BRUCE, JOHN, in Grenada, father of a son born 22 January 1817, [S.2.17], and a daughter born 10 January 1818, [DPCA.807],

BRUCE, JOHN, from Grenada, married Isabel Paterson, at 82 Great King Street, Edinburgh, on 17 April 1827. [BM.21.772]

BRUCE, J. S., born 1805, a Customs officer, son of S. B. Bruce a surgeon in Ripon, died in Grenada on 12 December 1833. [GM.104.454]

BRUCE, Sir MICHAEL, a planter on Shewan Estate, Tobago, in 1836. [TNA.T71.1572]

BRUCE, ROBERT GEORGE, an engineer in Dominica in 1776. [NRS.GD20.1.384]; probate 1779, PCC. [TNA]

BRUCE, THOMAS, in St Vincent, son of David Bruce of Kinnaird, died in Edinburgh on 24 January 1789. [GM.12.579.38]

BRUCE, WILLIAM, in Tobago, son of Sir Michael Bruce of Stenhouse, deeds, 1788, 1792. [NRS.RD3.247.683/RD3.257.361]

BRUGMAN, ..., a planter in Curacao around 1719.

BRUMANT, GEORGE, warden of St George's parish, Dominica, in 1847. [DC27.2.1847]

BRUMANT, PIERRE, constable in St Andrew's, Dominica, 1847. [DC:27.2.1847]

BRYDEN, JAMES, born 1811, son of David Bryden a millwright in Douglas, Lanarkshire, died in Trinidad on 21 December 1838. [SG.8.745]

BUBB, C. H., a merchant in St George's, Grenada, 1859. [DC:954]

BUCHAN, ALEXANDER, a merchant from Glasgow, died in Grenada on 3 July 1795. [GM.65.968]

BUCHAN, ROBERT, son of Robert Buchan in Chapel, Cambuslang, died in Tobago in 1817. [S.14.17]

THE PEOPLE OF THE WINDWARD ISLANDS, TRINIDAD AND TOBAGO, AND CURACAO, 1620 1860

BUCHANAN, ALEXANDER, a merchant from Glasgow, died in Grenada in 1795. [SM.57.682]

BUCHANAN, ALEXANDER, in Tobago, did 29 November 1807. [SM.70.398]

BUCHANAN, ALEXANDER, sometime in Tobago, later in Campbelltown, Argyll, edict of executry, 1811. 20 December 1811, Comm. Argyll. [NRS]

BUCHANAN, Reverend ARTHUR JOHN PILGRIM, in Carriacou, son of Captain Colin Buchanan of the 62nd Regiment, married Margaret Ann Jemitt, daughter of Francis Jemitt of Richmond Estate, Grenada, on 4 February 1847. [GM.ns27.542]

BUCKLEY, The Right Reverend JAMES, D.D., Bishop of Gerron, Apostolic of the British, Danish and Dutch West Indian Islands and Colonies, died in Trinidad on 24 March 1828. [DPCA.346]

BULL, ..., born 1735, a gentleman from London, emigrated via Plymouth aboard the Laurent bound for Grenada in January 1775. [TNA.T47.9/11]

BULLER, WILLIAM, Customs collector, also Colonel of the 1st Battalion of the Trinidad Militia, died in Trinidad on 10 June 1802. [GM.72.781][EA.4037]

BULLOCK, ELIZA, wife of Joseph Bullock the Commissary General of the West Indies, died in Martinique on 12 June 1809. [GM.79.679]

BURGESS, Mr, born 1748, a gentleman, via Plymouth aboard the Le Soy Planter bound for Dominica in 1774. [TNA.T47.9/11]

BURKE, EDMUND PLUNKETT, born 1805, late of the Inner Temple in London, and Caius College, Cambridge, a Judge in St Lucia, died in Dominica in 1835. [GM.105.222]

BURN, GEORGE PERCY, born 10 November in Roxburghshire, son of Reverend William Burn and his wife Margaret Ogle, died in Dominica in 1800. [F.2.133]

BURN, JOHN, in Dominica, a will, 13 January 1792. [NRS.RD3.292.419]; a deed, 12 January 1796. [NRS.RD3.292.1038]

BURNETT, ALEXANDER, son of ......Burnett of Elrick, died in Union near Grenada on 18 June 1790. [SM.52.464]

BURNETT, THEODOSIUS, in Dominica, brother of John Burnett a merchant in Aberdeen, 1783. [NRS.GD23.3.51]

BURNLEY, WILLIAM HARDIN, born 1780, died in Port of Spain, Trinidad, on 29 December 1850. [GM.ns35.334]

BURNS, ROBERT, a merchant, died in Trinidad on 20 October 1804. [SM.67.74]

BURNTFIELD, DAVID, born 1808, son of George Burntfield and his wife Lillie Stewart, died on 4 June 1838 in Dominica. [Greyfriars gravestone, Perth]

BURTON, JOSEPH, constable in St Andrew's, Dominica, 1847. [DC:27.2.1847]

BUSHE, ROBERT, born 1790, in Trinidad, died in London on 20 October 1844. [GM.ns22.664]

BUSHE AND DARLING, on St Vincent Wharf, Port of Spain, Trinidad, in 1843. [PSG.1806]

BUSHE, Reverend THOMAS FRANCIS, fourth son of Robert Bushe in Trinidad, died in Folkestone on 19 May 1858. [GM.ns2/4.681]

BUTTER, JOHN, born 1806, a surgeon from Bristol, settled in Trinidad, died in New York on 19 June 1848. [GM.ns30.447]

BYLES, MATHEW, in Grenada, probate, 1803, PCC. [TNA] [PSG.1806]

CACHETTE, PIERRE, constable of St Mark's, Dominica, in 1847. [DC.27.2.1847]

CALHOUN Brothers, merchants on St Vincent Wharf, Port of Spain, Trinidad, 1843. [PSG.1806]

CALVERT, EDWARD, a headmaster of Queen's School, Trinidad, married Emily Wisset, widow of A. Middleton, a marine surveyor, in London, on 17 February 1859. [GM.ns2/6.317]; she died in Port of Spain, Trinidad, on 4 September 1859. [GM.ns2/7.54]

CAMBRON, THEODORUS, a Dutch Reformed Church pastor in Curacao from 1714

CAMERON, ALEXANDER, born 1727, a cartwright from Drumnaglass, a Jacobite banished to the Leeward Islands, liberated by the French and landed on Martinique n 1747. [P.2.70][TNA.SP36.102]

CAMERON, ALEXANDER, Captain of the 6th West Indian Regiment, died in Dominica on 28 January 1813. [GM.83.660]

CAMERON, ANNE, born 1718, a spinner from Lochaber, a Jacobite banished to the Leeward Islands, liberated by the French and landed on Martinique in 1747. [P.2.72][TNA.SP36.102]

CAMERON, EFFIE, born 1718, a spinner in Lochaber, a Jacobite banished to the Leeward Islands, liberated by the French and landed on Martinique in 1747. [P.2.80][TNA.SP36.102]

CAMERON, FLORA, born 1706, a spinner in Lochaber, a Jacobite banished to the Leeward Islands, liberated by the French and landed on Martinique in 1747. [P.2.80][TNA.SP36.102]

CAMERON, JOHN, on Tempe Estate, Grenada, married Annette Baillie, only daughter of Evan Baillie a barrister, on 19 January 1852. [GM.ns37.509]

CAMPBELL, ALEXANDER, born 1707, a weaver in Argyll, a Jacobite banished to the Leeward Islands, liberated by the French and landed on Martinique in 1747. [P.2.88][TNA.SP36.102]

CAMPBELL, ALEXANDER, born 1720, a labourer in Argyll, a Jacobite banished to the Leeward Islands, liberated by the French and landed on Martinique in 1747. [P.2.88][TNA.SP36.102]

CAMPBELL, ALEXANDER, born 1731, a servant in Rannoch, a Jacobite banished to the Leeward Islands, liberated by the French and landed on Martinique in 1747. [P.2.94][TNA.SP36.102]

CAMPBELL, ALEXANDER, of Maran, Grenada, 1803. [NRS.GD112.61.2]

CAMPBELL, ANGUS, son of Campbell of Fornighty, a Captain of the 37th Regiment, died in St Vincent in 1801. [EEC.30.7.1801]

CAMPBELL, BARBARA, born 1727, a spinner in Argyll, a Jacobite banished to the Leeward Islands, liberated by the French and landed on Martinique in 1747. [P.2.88][TNA.SP36.102]

CAMPBELL, CHARLOTTE, in Tobago, probate, 1800, PCC. [TNA]

CAMPBELL, DONALDSON, in Grenada, 1795. [NRS.GD18.3532]

CAMPBELL, DOUGALL, born 1730, a servant in Lochaber, a Jacobite banished to the Leeward Islands, liberated by the French and landed on Martinique in 1747. [P.2.90][TNA.SP36.102]

CAMPBELL, DUNCAN, born 1730, a labourer in Argyll, a Jacobite banished to the Leeward Islands, liberated by the French and landed on Martinique in 1747. [P.2.90][TNA.SP36.102]

CAMPBELL, DUNCAN, in St Vincent, 1776. [NLS.Acc.8796.6]; in St Vincent, 1779, brother of Mary Campbell at Ardnave. [Argyll Sheriff Court Deeds, 21.6.1787]; died at Clifton on 15 September 1797. [GM.67.895]; probate, 1797, PCC. [TNA]

CAMPBELL, EDWARD, married Miss Jones of Jamaica, in Grenada in October 1800. [WHM.256]

CAMPBELL, GRACE, widow of Alexander Campbell in Tobago, died in Edinburgh on 12 December 1823. [DPCA.1078]

CAMPBELL, GRACE, fourth daughter of Angus Campbell of Maryhill, Tobago, and grand-daughter of Elphinstone Piggott the Chief Justice of Tobago, married Reverend Henry Martyn Capel, a school inspector, in Ryde, Isle of Wight on 23 August 1867. [GM.ns2/17.512]

CAMPBELL, HELEN, daughter of Mungo Campbell in Grenada, married John Campbell of Strachur, in St Andrew's Episcopa Church in Glasgow on 1 November 1787. [Scottish Antiquary.x.22]

CAMPBELL, ISABELLA, eldest daughter of Robert Campbell in Bridgend, Greenock, died at St Mary's Hill, Tobago, on 19 April 1834. [SG.252]

CAMPBELL, JAMES, born 1747, an attorney, from London aboard the Westerhall bound for the Grenades in December 1773. [TNA.T47.9-11]

CAMPBELL, JAMES, in Grenada, 1776. [NLS.Acc.8793.52]; a merchant in St George's, Grenada in 1782. [NRS.AC7.58]; in Grenada, probate, 1806, PCC. [TNA]

CAMPBELL, JAMES, formerly a planter in Tobago, later in Rothesay, testament, 1784, Comm. The Isles. [NRS]

CAMPBELL, JAMES, late in Tobago, died 29 March 1801. [EEC]

CAMPBELL, JAMES, of Ormaig, Captain of a troop of native cavalry during the late insurrection in St Vincent and Grenada, died 21 April 1805. [EEC]

CAMPBELL, JAMES, of Argyll Estate, Tobago, died 13 October 1805. [EEC][SM.68.78]

CAMPBELL, JAMES, late of Grenada, died 3 May 1810. [EEC]; inventory, 30 November 1810, Comm. Edinburgh. [NRS.SC70.1.3.252]

CAMPBELL, Dr JAMES S., a Member of the Council of Tobago, second son of Alexander Campbell an Excise Collector, died at Orangehill, Tobago, on 4 March 1824. [S.452.295]

CAMPBELL, JAMES, born 6 August 1829 at Moor Park, Lanarkshire, son of James Murdoch Campbell and his wife Elizabeth Bogle, died at Mount Pleasant, St Vincent, on 14 May 1845. [Dean gravestone, Edinburgh]

CAMPBELL, JAMES, from St Vincent, died in Polmont, Stirlingshire, on 20 May 1832. [EEC.18808]

CAMPBELL, JAMES, younger son of Gray Campbell, Golden Square, Aberdeen, died in Trinidad in July 1836. [AJ.4627]

CAMPBELL, JOHN, of Campbell, Rivers, and Company in Glasgow, died in Trinidad on 24 August 1817. [S.1.42]

CAMPBELL, Sir JOHN, of Ardnamurchan, the Lieutenant Governor of St Vincent, died 18 January 1853. [St Vincent gravestone]

CAMPBELL, JOHN, born 1726, a labourer in Inverness, a Jacobite banished to the Leeward Islands, liberated by the French and landed on Martinique in 1747. [P.2.94][TNA.SP36.102]

CAMPBELL, JOHN ALEXANDER, born 1762 in Scotland, lately of Tobago, died in St John, New Brunswick, on 19 August 1800. [RGNA]

CAMPBELL, JOHN, a merchant in Tobago, 1776. [TNA.T1.527.271-272]

CAMPBELL, JOHN, late in Grenada, later in Perth, son of John Campbell a merchant in Perth, testament, 1796, Comm. St Andrews. [NRS]

CAMPBELL, Sir JOHN, born 27 November 1807, son of Sir John Campbell the Lieutenant Governor of St Vincent, died in Kingstown, St Vincent, on 18 January 1853. [GM.ns39.542]

CAMPBELL, LACHLAN, son of Campbell of Craignish, died on passage home from Tobago, edict of executry, 1785. [NRS.CC2.8.88/6]

CAMPBELL, LUCY, widow of Duncan Forbes Sutherland of St Vincent, married John Hall, MD, at the Cape of Good Hope on 31 October 1848. [SG.1786]

CAMPBELL, LYDIA, a planter on Lower Quarter Estate, Tobago, in 1836. [TNA.T71.1572]

CAMPBELL, MARK, only son of Dr Alexander Campbell in Dunkeld, died in Grenada on 2 December 1791. [GCr.90][EEC.11522]

CAMPBELL, MUNGO, brother of Colin Campbell of Strachur, emigrated to Grenada by 1787, late in Grenada, later in Edinburgh, was admitted as a burgess and guilds-brother of Ayr on 2 October 1780, died in 1793. [ABR][NNQ.X.22]

CAMPBELL, PATRICK, in Tobago, a deed of factory, 3 July 1775. [NRS.RD2.217/2.268]

CAMPBELL, PETER, the Lieutenant Governor of Tobago, died on 9 January 1779. [SM.41.79]

CAMPBELL, STIRLING, son of George Campbell of Ellister, Islay, died in Grenada in 1795. [SM.57.612]

CAMPBELL, THOMAS, born 1745, a planter, from Plymouth aboard the Albion bound for St Vincent in 1775. [TNA.T47.9/11]

CAMPBELL, THOMAS, a merchant in Grenada, 1790, [NRS.0623.TMJ.427.36]; owner of the Betsy of Glasgow, 1793, [NRS.CE60.11.3.13]; died in Demerara on 14 May 1795. [EEC.23.7.1795]

CAMPBELL, WILLIAM, born 1725, a weaver in Perthshire, a Jacobite banished to the Leeward Islands, liberated by the French and landed on Martinique in 1747. [P.2.98][TNA.SP36.102]

CAMPBELL, WILLIAM, died in St Vincent on 7 June 1839. [SG.8.805]

CAMPBELL, ..., son of Sir George Campbell of Ardnamurchan, was born in St Vincent on 27 January 1845. [PC.2010]

CAMPBELL, BLANE, and Company, merchants in Grenada in 1782. [NRS.CS17.1.1]

CAMPE, Reverend CHARLES, in Port of Spain, Trinidad, only son of Charles Campe in Esses, Trinidad, married Rebecca Sharpe, daughter of John Sharpe in Maidstone, Kent, on 15 April 1847. [GM.ns28.198]

CANTFORT, JAMES, an 'interpreter' in Otra Banda, Curacao, in 1812. [CGCA.:11.12.1812]

CARMICHAEL, MARGARETTA JANE, second daughter of John Wilson Carmichael, late Captain of the 53rd Regiment, married Pemberton Hobson, a barrister at law, in St Vincent on 1 August 1821. [BM.10.35 8]

CARMICHAEL, THOMAS, son of Thomas Carmichael a merchant in Greenock and his wife Agnes Orr, died in Trinidad on 18 April 1838. [Greenock West gravestone]

CARREW, Mr., a planter in the Grenades, from Portsmouth aboard the Friendship bound for the Grenades in April 1774. [TNA.T47.9-11]

CARRICK, Mr, a merchant, from Portsmouth to Tobago aboard the Unity in April 1775. [TNA.T47.9-11]

CARSON, ROBERT, born 1754, a surgeon in London, emigrated via London aboard the Simond bound for the Grenades in November 1774. [TNA.T47.9/11]

CARUTH, ANDREW, born 1783, died in Goldsburgh, Tobago, on 30 August 1844. [SG.1342]

THE PEOPLE OF THE WINDWARD ISLANDS, TRINIDAD AND TOBAGO, AND CURACAO, 1620 1860

CATTENACH, ALEXANDER, born 1730, a miller in Badenoch, a Jacobite banished to the Leeward Islands, liberated by the French and landed on Martinique in 1747. [P.2.104][TNA.SP36.102]

CAZALEY, LEWIS, born 1746, a surgeon in London, emigrated via London aboard the Hero bound for the Grenades in February 1774. [TNA.T47.9-11]

CHADBAND, J., ADC to the Governor, died in Tobago in 1831. [GM.101.652]

CHALLET, SAMUEL, Customs Collector, died in Trinidad on 13 May 1814. [GM.84.189]

CHALMERS, ALEXANDER SCOTT, from Aberdeenshire, died in Rutland Vale, St Vincent, on 9 January 1863. [AF.18.2.1863]

CHALMERS, ISABEL, born 1722, a knitter from the Mearns, a Jacobite banished to the Leeward Islands, liberated by the French and landed on Martinique in 1747. [P.2.108][TNA.SP36.102]

CHALMERS, JOHN, born 1725, a labourer from Perthshire, a Jacobite banished to the Leeward Islands, liberated by the French and landed on Martinique in 1747. [P.2.110][TNA.SP36.102]

CHALMERS, THOMAS, Customs Collector, died in Tobago on 5 October 1801. [GM.71.1211]

CHALMERS, WILLIAM, born 1780, son of John Chalmers of Westfield and his wife Agnes Forbes, died in Dominica on 5 July 1811. [NRS.NRAS.3626.970][NRS.GD171.970][Old Aberdeen gravestone][AJ.5.7.1811]

CHAMBERS, CAROLINE DARRACOTT, eldest daughter of James Chambers a colonial revenue officer, died in Grenada on 1 August 1863. [S.2560]

29

CHAMPION, JOHN CAREY, born 1787, Major of the 21st Regiment, the Royal Scots Fusiliers, died 13 October 1824. [St Vincent gravestone]

CHANCE, JANE, born 1739, a planter from Jamaica, bound from London to Grenada aboard the Rochard in March 1774. [TNA.T47.9-11]

CHAPMAN, GEORGE, assistant staff surgeon to the Forces, eldest son of L. Chapman in Crieff, died in St Vincent on 25 August 1839. [EEC.19977]

CHAPMAN, WILLIAM, born 1715, a pedlar in Aberdeenshire, a Jacobite banished to the Leeward Islands, liberated by the French and landed on Martinique in 1747. [P.2.110][TNA.SP36.102]

CHARITIE, PHILIP, a merchant, from London bound for the Grenades aboard the Grenada Galley in June 1774. [TNA.T47.9-11]

CHASOT, ST ROSE, warden of St Patrick's parish, Dominica, 1847. [DC27.2.1847]

CHAUNCY, CHARLES S., in Grenada, probate, 1809, PCC. [TNA]

CHECKLEY, Reverend JOHN, born on 31 March 1789 in Cork, educated at Trinity College, Dublin, died 6 January 1852. [St Vincent gravestone]

CHERPI, GABRIEL, in Grenada in 1769. [JCTP.1769.156]

CHILD, WILLIAM ARNDALE, a Writer to the Signet, stipendiary magistrate of Tobago, died there on 20 October 1861. [S.1999][TNA.CO290.4]

CHISHOLM, Dr, from Grenada, married Eliza Cooper, daughter of John Cooper in St Kitts, in Inverness on 22 December 1794. [EA.3235.422]

CHOLLETT, SAMUEL, a Loyalist in Charleston, South Carolina, settled in Dominica by 1784. [TNA.AO13.97.262-266]

CHOPPIN, CAROLINE, eldest daughter of James Choppin in St Vincent, married James Protheroe from Bristol, in Bath on 27 August 1806. [GM.76.873]

CHRISTIE, JAMES ANDREW, in St Lucia, probate, 1806, PCC. [TNA]

CHRISTIE, WILLIAM, born 16 December 1817, son f John Christie and his wife Janet Jamieson in Kincardine-on-Forth, died in Port of Spain, Trinidad, on 4 July 1838. [Tulliallan gravestone]

CLAIRMONTE, JOHN L., King Street, Kingstown, St Vincent, 1870. [SVW:11.8.1870]

CLAPHAM, Reverend JOHN HENRY, died in Port of Spain, Trinidad, on 3 January 1835. [GM.105.441]

CLAPPERTON, WILLIAM, born 1733, a ploughboy, a Jacobite banished to the Leeward Islands, liberated by the French and landed on Martinique in 1747. [P.2.116][TN A.SP36.102]

CLARK, ANN ELIZA, eldest daughter of James Clark, MD, in Dominica, married John Sim MD, in London on 9 October 1817. [GM.87.466]

CLARK, JAMES, a surgeon in Dominica, Dominica, graduated MD from King's College, Aberdeen, on 17 September 1773. [KCA.134]; in Dominica, a sasine, 18 August 1783. [NRS.RS.Aberdeen.194]

CLARK, OSWALD, in Tobago, 1 July 1797, [NRS.RD3.292.330]; probate, 1802, PCC. [TNA]

CLARK, Dr JAMES, a surgeon in Dominica, graduated MD at King's College, Aberdeen, on 17 September 1773. [KCA.134]; in Dominica, a sasine, 18 August 1783. [NRS.RS.Aberdeen .194]; a former Councillor of Dominica, died in London on 21 January 1819. [GM.88.184]

CLARK, JOHN, born 1739, from Tobago, died in Berwick-on-Tweed on 24 January 1807. [GM.77.185]

CLARK, Mr., born 1736, a gentleman, via Plymouth aboard the Le Soy Planter bound for Dominica in 1774. [TNA.T47.9/11]

CLAVERING, Mrs ELIZABETH HAMILTON or, born 1724, a seamstress in Banff, a Jacobite banished to the Leeward Islands, liberated by the French and landed on Martinique in 1747. [P.2.118][TNA.SP36.102]

CLAY, CHARLES, from Northumberland, died in Trinidad on 13 March 1807. [SM.69.477]

CLELAND, WILLIAM, in Martinique, 1729, son of Robert Cleland of Pedenie and his wife Jane Henderson. [NRS.GD172.978]

CLOOTS, PIETER, a Jesuit in Curacao around 1738

CLOUET, ELIZABETH, in St Vincent in 1777. [JCTP.84.69]

CLOZIER, ..., born 1753, a planter from London, emigrated aboard the Proudfoot bound via Plymouth for Grenada in October 1774. [TNA.T47.9/11]

COATS, WILLIAM, born 1691, a labourer in Aberdeenshire, a Jacobite banished to the Leeward Islands, liberated by the French and landed on Martinique in 1747. [P.2.120][TNA.SP36.102]

COCHRANE, ANDREW, late Governor of Dominica, died in 1833. [NRS.GD172.644]

COCKBURN, ALEXANDER, born 1738, a planter from London, with his wife born 1748, via Plymouth aboard the Lawrent bound for Dominica in January 1774. [TNA.T47.9-11]

COCKBURN, Reverend HENRY, born 1801 in Haddington, educated at Edinburgh University, minister of St Andrews, Grenada in 1838, married Mary, daughter of Charles Ritchie a merchant in Edinburgh, in Grenada on 22 August 1839. [SG.8.813]; he died there on 19 July 1854. [EEC.22622][F.7.667]

COCKBURN, JOHN, in Dominica in 1776. [NLS.Acc.8793]

COCKBURN, WALTER, a planter on St Mary Hill Estate, Tobago, in 1836. [TNA.T71.1572]

COCKBURN, Miss, eldest daughter of Dr Alexander Cockburn in Grenada, married William Baillie Rose, in Edinburgh on 23 April 1798. [GM.68.441]

COERMAN, HERMAN, fiscal of Curacao in 1760s

COHEN, SAMUEL, born in Portugal, moved to Holland, settled in Curacao from 1634 to 1642.

COLDSTREAM, ALEXANDER, manager of Mitcham Estate in Dominica, eldest son of Alexander Coldstream in St Andrews, Fife, in 1799. [NRS.B65.5.8.104-106]

COLEBROOKE, Sir WILLIAM, Governor in Chief of Tobago in 1849.

COLQUHOUN, WALTER, married Miss MacAlister, in Logan, Dominica, in 1776. [GM.46.435]

COMBAUD, PIERRE, a Jesuit at La Grande Savanne, St Vincent in 1686. [SPAWI.1686.871xii]

COMBE, NICOLAAS, a customs clerk and planter in Curacao in 1760s

CONNOR, CHARLES, born 1751, a merchant in London, from London aboard the Noble bound for Dominica in April 1775. [TNA.T47.9/11]

CONSTANT, PIETER, Governor of Tobago in 1672. [SPAWI.1672.995]

CONWAY, LUKE, in Dominica, probate, 1807, PCC. [TNA]

COPLAND, JOHN, born in Ellon, Aberdeenshire, in 1812, died at Tufton Hall, Grenada, on 16 May 1870. [AJ.22.6.1870]

CORAM, JAMES CHOPPIN, born 1809, died 16 June 1858. [St Vincent gravestone]

CORBETT, WALTER, in St Vincent, a deed, 1774. [NRS.GD514.1.33.6]; brother of John Corbett of Tollcross, died in St Vincent on 4 September 1786. [GM.IX.465.382][SM.48.622]

CORLET, JAMES, Speaker of the Assembly of Dominica, Lieutenant Colonel of the St George Militia Regiment, died 1840. [GM.ns14.676]

CORRIE, THOMAS, a planter on Lower Quarter Estate, Tobago, in 1836. [TNA.T71.1572]

CORRIE, MCALISTER, & Co., in Trinidad, 1846. [TS.1.1.1846]

CORSAR, FREDERICK, born 1739, a planter, with his wife born 1744, and a child, bound from Plymouth aboard the Westerhall for the Grenades in January 1774. [TNA.T47.9-11]

COTINO, ABRAHAM HENRIQUES, a merchant in Curacao in 1747. [NAN.OAC.179/10]

COTINO, Captain MOSSEH HENRIQUES, a ship-owner in Willemsted, Curacao, in 1753, died 1762. [Beth Haim gravestone, Curacao]

COTTER, PETER, born 1815, died in Belle Plane, St Lucia, on 2 December 1842. [GM.ns19.556]

COULL, J.G., a merchant in Kingston, St Vincent, 1870. [SVW:11.8.1870]

COULL, WILLIAM, from St Vincent, died in Cullen, Banffshire, on 30 September 1815. [GM.85.635]

COULTER, DAVID, son of William Coulter [1805-1875] and his wife Mary McBride [1810-1863], died in Trinidad aged 34. [Ballantrae gravestone]

COURNEUVE, LEWIS DU MOULIN, in Dominica in 1771. [JCTP.78.188]

COURT, CHARLES, born 1756, a planter from London, emigrated via Plymouth aboard the Lovely Betsy bound for Dominica in March 1774. [TNA.T47.9-11]

COWIE, DAVID, born 1826, son of Reverend William Cowie in Cairney, Aberdeenshire, died in St Vincent on 8 January 1878. [AJ.26.1.1878]; his daughter was born in St Vincent on 30 April 1867. [GM.ns3/4.98]

CRABTREE, SCOTT, and Company, shipping agents on South Quay, Port of Spain, Trinidad, 1843. [PSG.1806]

CRAIG, Mr, a planter in Tobago, died in London in November 1794. [GM.ns1060]

CRANSTOUN, Lord JAMES, Governor of Grenada, died in Fareham on 22 August 1796. [GM.66.798]

CRAWFORD, JAMES, born 1776, son of Daniel Crawford and his wife Janet Hunter, died in Grenada in 1803. [Cumbrae gravestone]

CRAWFORD, JOHN R., from 53 Lilybank Road, Glasgow, died on the Shirvan Estate, Tobago, on 28 July 1875. [EC.28366]

CRAWFORD, JOSEPH, born 1777, son of Daniel Crawford and his wife Janet Hunter, died in Grenada in 1803. [Cumbrae gravestone]

CRICHTON, JAMES, a merchant in Martinique, reference in Thomas Turnbull's testament, 1817.

CROOKS, THOMAS, son of Thomas Crooks and his wife Christian Cormack, a planter in Tobago in 1803. [Dun gravestone, Angus]

CROOKS, WILLIAM, MD, in Tobago, son of Thomas Crooks and his wife Christian Cormack in Dun, Angus, died on passage from Tobago and America in 1802, [Dun gravestone]; probate, 1811, PCC. [TNA]

CROOKS, WILLIAM, a planter on Belmont Estate, Tobago, in 1836. [TNA.T71.1572]

CRUICKSHANK, CATHERINE, youngest daughter of Dr James Cruickshank in Haughs of Corse, Aberdeenshire, married John Hope, a surgeon, at Mount Pleasant Church, Tobago, on 16 March 1844. [AJ.5023]

CRUICKSHANK, COSMO G., son of Dr Cruickshank of Haughs, Forgue, Aberdeenshire, died on Mount St George Estate, Tobago, on 31 August 1853. [AJ.12.10.1853]

CRUICKSHANK, EMMA JANE, daughter of John Cruickshank of Prospect Estate, Tobago, married Kayr Dowland, in Tobago, on 29 October 1845. [AJ.5109]

CRUICKSHANK, JAMES, of Richmond, St Vincent, married Margaret Helen Gerard, youngest daughter of Dr Alexander Gerard, Professor of Divinity at King's College, Aberdeen, in Strathcathro, Angus, on 25 June 1792. [GCr.131]; he was granted Langley Park, Scotland, on 20 December 1793. [NRS.RGS.127.111]

CRUICKSHANK, JAMES, an indentured servant, bound for Carriacou, the Grenadines, in 1804. [PSAS.114.499]

CRUICKSHANK, JOHN, born 1732, a herdsman from Aberdeen, a Jacobite banished to the Leeward Islands, liberated by the French and landed on Martinique in 1747. [P.2.138][TNA.SP36.102]

CRUICKSHANKS, JOHN, born 1766, from St Vincent, died in Coupar Angus, Perthshire, on 29 July 1810. [EA.4863.87]

CRUICKSHANK, JOHN, born 1792, son of Dr Cruickshank of Haughs, Forgue, a member of the Council of Tobago, died there on 20 August 1850. [AJ.23.10.1850]

THE PEOPLE OF THE WINDWARD ISLANDS, TRINIDAD AND TOBAGO, AND CURACAO, 1620-1860

CRUICKSHANK, LAURENCE MUDIE, in Tobago, son of Dr Cruickshank in the Haughs of Corse, Aberdeenshire, died on passage from Tobago to Demerara on 14 June 1849. [AJ.5299][EEC.21850]

CRUICKSHANK, PATRICK, from St Vincent, married [1] Peggy Davidson from Newcastle, in Edinburgh on 3 December 1775, and [2] Jane Chambers, daughter of the Customs Collector of Leith, in Edinburgh on 1 May 1780. [EMR]

CRUICKSHANK, PATRICK, from St Vincent, married Clementina Houston, eldest daughter of Alexander Houston, in Grantown in 1813. [EA.5182.13]

CULLOW, JAMES, son of Reverend John Cullow in Penpont, died in Tobago in 1796. [SM.58.218]

CUMMING, EMILY, daughter of A. Cumming in St Vincent, married J. M. Grant a Lieutenant of the Royal Engineers, son of, Colonel Grant of the Royal Artillery, on 19 April 1849. [GM.ns32.84][EEC.21815]

CUMMING, MARGARET, third daughter of Alexander Cumming in Rabacco, St Vincent, married Caledon Richard Egerton, a Captain of the 89th Regiment, in Trinity Church, Georgetown, St Vincent, on 30 May 1843. [GM.ns20..199][AJ.4956]

CUMMING, JAMES, born 1811, son of William Cumming a merchant in Inverness, and his wife Marjory McHardy, died in St Vincent in 1832. [Llanbryde gravestone]

CUMMING, JOSEPH, in Carriacou by Grenada, testament 3 July 1799, Comm. Edinburgh. [NRS]

CUMMINS, SARAH, second daughter of George Cummins, the Archdeacon of Trinidad, married Lord George Francis Harris the Governor of Trinidad, there on 16 April 1850. [GM.ns34.200]

CUNNINGHAM, ALEXANDER FAIRLIE, second son of Sir William Cunningham of Robertland, died in Tobago on 30 June 1795. [GM.65.791][SM.57.612]

CUNNINGHAM, CHARLES, in Grenada in 1784. [NRS.GD237.217.3]

CUNNINGHAM, GEORGE, a resident of Curacao in 1735. [Brieven en Papieren van Curacao.]

CUNNINGHAM, JOHN, born 1715 in Argyll, a Jacobite banished to the Leeward Islands, liberated by the French and landed on Martinique in 1747. [P.2.140][TNA.SP36.102]

CUNNINGHAM, JOHN, born 1779, son of Thomas Cunningham a painter in Edinburgh, died in Dominica in May 1803. [SM.66.566]

CUNNINGHAM, SAMUEL, jr., a merchant in St Vincent and Martinique, letters, 1792-1796. [PRONI.DOD.1108/3-11, 16-17]

CUNNINGHAM, WILLIAM, from Glasgow, died in Trinidad on 13 October 1819. [BM.7.119][EEC.16971]

CUNNINGHAM, WILLIAM, a shipping agent on King's Wharf, Port of Spain, Trinidad, 1843. [PSG.1806]

CURRIE, ARCHIBALD, a merchant in New York, died in Martinique in 1803. [EA .4048]

CURRIE, DONALD, born 1850, died in Tobago in March 1868. [Clachan gravestone, Arran]

CURRIE, THOMAS, in Lowlands, Tobago, died in 1801. [GM.71.576][GC.1533]

CURTIS, ROGER WILLIAM, third son of Admiral Sir Lucius Curtis in East Cosham, Hampshire, died in Trinidad, on 23 September 1859. [GM.ns2/7.654]

CUSHNY, ARTHUR, born 31 August 1797, eldest son of Reverend Cushny in Oyne, Aberdeenshire, educated at King's College, Aberdeen, in 1801, a merchant in Trinidad, died in 1811. [SM.73.637][KCA.2.388]

DAKINS, LYDIA, widow of Thomas Dakins in Trinidad, died in Pembury, Kent, on 6 December 1843. [GM.ns21.107]

DALLAS, COLIN, in St Vincent, died 26 January 1810, [GM.80.91]; probate, 1810, PCC. [TNA]

DALLAS, GEORGE, son of John Dallas in Glasgow, died in Trinidad on 26 June 1802. [EA.4039.02]

DALRYMPLE, HUGH, the Attorney General of Grenada, died 9 March 1774. [GM.44.239]

DALRYMPLE, JAMES, fourth son of William Dalrymple in Tullos, died in Dominica on 24 September 1821. [AJ.3860]

DALRYMPLE, JAMES, of Bathazard Estate, Grenada, died in 1851. [S.24.1.1852]

DALZELL, JOHN, born 1782, Speaker of the Assembly of St Vincent, died 11 October 1829. [St Vincent gravestone]

DALZIEL, JOHN, in Grenada, letters, 1773-1774. [EUL.ms.DK.52/19/34/53/60/61]

DANIELL, THOMAS, born 1753, Attorney General of Dominica, died at Snettisham, King's Lynn, Norfolk, on 17 March 1806. Snettisham gravestone][GM.76.293]

DANIELL, Miss, only daughter of Thomas Daniell, the Attorney General of Dominica, married John Holmes jr. from Belfast, in Snesham, Norfolk, on 1 April 1802. [GM.72.373]

THE PEOPLE OF THE WINDWARD ISLANDS, TRINIDAD AND TOBAGO, AND CURACAO, 1620-1860

DARLING, ANN WILHELMINA, born 1813, eldest daughter of Allan Dalzell, wife of Lieutenant C. H. Darling of the 57th Regiment, died in Government House, Tobago, on 16 October 1837. [GM.ns9.222]

DARLING, Major General HENRY CHARLES, Lieutenant Governor of Tobago, died there on 7 September 1835. [GM.ns5.317]

DARLINGTON, SAMUEL, from Tobago, died at Cornhill on 18 November 1777. [GM.48.551]

DASENT, Reverend ALEXANDER, fourth son of J. R. Dasent the Attorney General of St Vincent, married Caroline Mayer Grant, second daughter of George Colquhoun Grant, in St Vincent, on 13 October 1847. [GM.ns29.80]

DASENT, ANN EMILY, eldest daughter of R. Dasent, the Attorney General, married Robert Aitken, in St Vincent on 13 October 1847. [GM.ns29.80]

DASENT, GEORGE WEBBE, third son of John Roche Dasent the Attorney General of St Vincent, married Frances Louisa Delane, third daughter of W. F. A. Delane, in London on 4 April 1846. [GM.ns25.639]

DASART, JOHN ROCHE, born 1796, late President of the Council and Attorney General of St Vincent, died 14 February 1832. [St Vincent gravestone]

DAUBERMINY, JEAN PIERRE, in Dominica in 1771. [JCTP.1773.274]

D'AUGLEBARME, HENRIETTA, daughter of John Peter D'Auglebarme, niece of Charles Bertrand, married Dugald Stewart Laidlaw, in Dominica on 10 December 1829. [S.1056.120]

DAVID, ELIZABETH, in St Vincent, dead by 1772. [JCTP.1772.319]

40

DAVIDSON, ALEXANDER, born 1729, a herdsman from Lochaber, a Jacobite banished to the Leeward Islands, liberated by the French and landed on Martinique in 1747. [TNA.SP36.102][P.2.144]

DAVIDSON, ANDREW, a surgeon from Aberdeen, brother of Thomas Davidson of Harvey Vale in the island, died in Carraciou near Grenada, on 3 November 1802. [EA.4082.03]

DAVIDSON, ANDREW, a surgeon, died in Grenada in March 1805. [SM.67.565][AJ.2991]

DAVIDSON, Dr CHARLES, son of John Davidson of Tillychetly, was educated at King's College, Aberdeen, 1790-1794, a physician who died in St George, Grenada, on 2 October 1804. [GM.74.1242][SM.67.74][KCA.2.371]

DAVIDSON, GEORGE, a surgeon in St Vincent, a sasine in 1784. [NRS.RS.Renfrew.1350]

DAVIES, MATTHEW, a merchant in Grenada, witness to deeds in 1819. [NRS.RD5.159.216/157.493]

DAVISON, CRAWFORD, a planter on Anoes Vale Estate, Tobago, in 1836. [TNA.T71.1572]

DAWES, WILLIAM, of Tuftonhall, Grenada, a Lieutenant of the Royal Navy, died in St George, Grenada, on 14 April 1819. [GM.88.585]

DEADY, Captain, of Cork, 'several years on the West India trade', died in Dominica in 1765. [FDJ.4023]

DE AMBLIMONT, Marquis, Governor of Martinique in 1698. [SPAWI.1698.1054/1089]

DE BEAUCHAMP, BOURKE, in Dominica in 1771. [JCTP.1773.274]

DE BIJ, WILLEM, Commissioner of the Slave Trade in Curacao in 1714

DE BLENAC, le Comte, Governor of Martinique 1678-1679. [SPAWI.1678,741ix; 1679.871]

DE BOMPAR, Marquis, Governor of Martinique, letters, 1750. [JCTP.1750-1751, 151/185]

DE CASEREZ, ABIGAYL, died in Curacao on 20 November 1742. [Beth Hain Cemetery, Curacao]

DE CASSARES, SEMUEL HISQUIA, died in Curacao on 16 April 1760. [Beth Hain Cemetery, Curacao]

DE CASTRO, ABRAHAM MENDES, a merchant in Curacao, died 1752, will.

DE CLERMONT DIEL, ..., Governor of Martinique in 1663. [CSPC.1663.578/581/617]

DE CLUGNY, AMELIA CONSTANCE GERTRUDE ETIENNETTE, only child of the late Baron de Clugny the Governor of Guadaloupe, widow of Raymond Godet, married Andrew Cochrane Johnston, son of the late Earl of Dundonald, son-in-law of the Earl of Hopetoun, in Martinique on 21 March 1803. [GM.73.689]

DA COSTA, ISAAC, a Dutch Sephardie, settled in Curacao in 1659, he brought 70 settlers from Amsterdam.

DE COURCERAC, Lieutenant, in Martinique in 1751. [JCTP.1751.185]

DE ESTAGES, JEAN BAPTISTE HUYGHUE, in Martinique, probate. 1804, PCC. [TNA]

DA FONSECA, JACOB LOPEZ, born in Curacao, educated at the Ets Chaim seminary in Amsterdam, rabbi in Curacao from 1764 until his death in 1815,

DE DONSECA, JOSEPH NUNES, alias DAVID NASSI, from Amsterdam to Curacao in 1653.

DE FONSECA, IEDITH NUNES, died in Curacao on 18 January 1668.
[Beth Hain Cemetery, Curacao]

DE FONSECA, JACOB NUNES, a planter in Curacao in 1682.

DE FONSEKOU, ISAECK, a merchant trading between Curacao and
Barbados in 1656.

DE GARNE, JEAN, born 1745, a planter from London, with his wife
born 1748, aboard the Reward bound from Plymouth to Grenada in
January 1775. [TNA.T47.9/11]

DE GLAPION, ..., born 1751, a planter from London, emigrated
aboard the Proudfoot bound via Plymouth for Grenada in October
1774. [TNA.T47.9/11]

DE GUITANDE, ..., Governor of Martinique in 1701.
[SPAWI.101.1192]

DE JOUX, Reverend J. G., in Dominica in 1840. [DC:1.8.1840]

DE LA BARRE, ..., Governor of Martinique in 1669. [SPAWI.1668-
1669,19/39/56/etc]

DE LA FENELON, ..., in Martinique in 1763. [JCTP.1763.384]

DE LA FOREST, Father CHARLES, in Martinique in 1689.
[SPAWI.1689.157iv]

DE LANCEY, STEPHEN, late Chief Justice of the Bahamas, Governor of
Tobago, died in December 1798. [GM.69.165]

DE LA PAGERIE, Madame, mother of Madame Buonaparte, died in
Martinique on 1 July 1807 and was buried in Les Trois Islets.
[GM.77.888]

DE LA POER-BERESFORD, HENRY CLEMENT, of the 69th Regiment,
youngest son of John De La Poer-Beresford, the Colonial Secretary of

St Vincent, married Matilda Hincks, youngest daughter of Francis
Hincks, the Governor of the Windward Islands, in Barbados on 23
July 1857. [GM.ns2/3.456]

DE LA RIVIERE, ..., in Martinique in 1763. [JCTP.1763.384]

DE LEON, JACOB HISQUIA, a merchant in Curacao, died 1760.

DELMESTRE, FRANCIS, in Dominica in 1772. [JCTP.1772.319]

DELMESTRE, PIERRE, in Dominica in 1772. [JCTP.1772.319]

DE MEY, PIETER, a shipmaster in Curacao in 1710, residing in
Pietermaai near Fort Amsterdam, Curacao in 1715.

DE MORG, CORNELIUS, a settler on Tobago before 1637. [HS.2nd
series, vol.171.113]

DE PAS FEUQUIRES, ..., Governor of Martinique and the French
Leeward Islands in 1721. [SPAWI.1721.501.viii]

DE PETERSON, JACOB, a merchant on Curacao in 1730s

DE POUY, JEAN, in St Vincent in 1777, [JCTP.84.69]

DE RAVINIER, LOUIS FOURNIER, in Grenada in 1769. [JCTP.1769.156]

DERAIGNY, Marquis, Governor of Martinique in 1691.
[SPAWI.1691.1557]

DE RUE, BALTHAZAR, in Curacao in 1677. [PCCol.1679.1246]

DE SOLA, JAHACOB, died in Curacao, 30 September 1812. [Beth Hain
Cemetery, Curacao]

DES BAT, JEAN, in Carriacou in 1771. [JCTP.1771.244]

DES BAT, LOUIS, in Carriacou in 1771. [JCTP.1771.244]

DES CHAMPS, ..., born 1735, a planter from London, aboard the Reward bound from Plymouth to Grenada in January 1775. [TNA.T47.9/11]

DES FONTAINES, JOHN LEWIS PAULIN, in Dominica in 1771. [JCTP.78.188]

DES MAGES, ..., in Grenada in 1763. [JCTP.1763.386]

DES NELL, DU PLESSIS ...., in St Vincent in 1772. [JCTP.1772.319]

D'ESNOS, ..., in Martinique in 1704. [SPAWI.1705.1025i]

DES RUAUX, ..., in St Lucia in 1731. [SPAWI.1731.248]

DE RUVYNES, LOUIS, in Martinique, probate, 1801, PCC. [TNA]

DE SAINT CROIX, JEAN JACQUES COQUILLE, in Martinique, probate, 1802, PCC. [TNA]

DE VALE, ELIAH, a planter in Curacao in 1680.

DE VEER, JOHAN, Governor of Curacao in 1783, 1795.

DE VOCONNU, PAUL MIGNOT, in Grenada in 1770. [JCTP.1770.180]

DE YLLAN, JAGO, born 1609 in Portugal, a merchant in Amsterdam, later in Curacao from 1652 to 1655.

DEWAR, ANDREW, Customs Collector, services of heirs, 1767, [NRS]; died in Dominica on 19 July 1771. [SM.33.503]

DEWAR, GEORGE, in St Kitts and in Dominica, probate 1786, PCC. [TNA]

DICK, COLIN MCKENZIE, of Los Efforts Estate, married Jane Finlay, daughter of Robert Finlay manager of the West Indian Bank, in San Fernando, Trinidad, on 18 August 1859. [EEC.23417]

DICK, JOSEPHINE R., in Port of Spain, Trinidad, 1846. [TS:1.1.1846]

DICK, ROBERT, a merchant in Trinidad, 1838, a deed, [NRS.RD5.596.65]; in 1839. [NRS.SC48.25.165]

DICK, ..., son of Colin McKenzie Dick, was born in San Fernando, Trinidad, on 16 May 1863. [S.2494]

DICK, ..., daughter of Colin McKenzie Dick, was born in San Fernando, Trinidad, on 30 May 1867. [S.2494]

DIDIER, CADET, constable in St Patrick's, Dominica, 1847. [DC.27.2.1847]

DINGWALL, DANIEL, born 1715, a glover in Inverness, a Jacobite banished to the Leeward Islands, liberated by the French and landed on Martinique in 1747. [P.2.154][TNA.SP36.102]

DISABIE, EDMOND, a gentleman, returning to his plantation in Dominica in October 1775 aboard the Darlington from Portsmouth. [TNA.T47.9/11]

DODS, JOHN, an engineer in Trinidad, testament, 1865. [NRS.SC70.1.126.393]

DODSON, THOMAS, in Martinique, probate, 1808, PCC. [TNA]

DOMVILE, Captain J. RUSSELL, the Customs Collector of Trinidad, son of Reverend H. B. Domvile in Pencombe, Herefordshire, died in Trinidad on 1 May 1853. [GM.ns40.98]

DONAUGHO, ELIZABETH, born 1752, emigrated via London aboard the Diana bound for Dominica in April 1774. [TNA.T47.9-11]

DONAUGHO, JOHN, born 1743, a planter from London, emigrated via London aboard the Diana bound for Dominica in April 1774. [TNA.T47.9-11]

DONALD, JAMES, born 1727, a tailor in the Mearns, a Jacobite transported to the Leeward Islands, liberated by the French and landed on Martinique in 1747. [P.2.156][TNA.SP36.102]

DONALDSON, ALEXANDER, an attorney, late of Grenada, died in Tobago in 1852. [S.6.3.1852]

DONALDSON, PETER, born 1740, a mason from Edinburgh, via London aboard the Greyhound bound for Dominica in December 1773. [TNA.T47.9-11]

DONCKER, JAN, merchant and Governor of Curacao, 16……

DOUGLAS, GEORGE, constable in St Patrick's, Dominica, 1847. [DC:27.2.1847]

DOUGLAS, JAMES ROBERT, born 1825, son of Archibald Douglas an advocate, died in Besquia, St Vincent, on 8 November 1849. [SG.18.1885]

DOUGLAS, JOHN, the Provost Marshal of Grenada, married Ellen Hardey of Brixton Hill, in Brixton on 2 January 1837, [GM.ns7.201]; he died in Grenada on 31 July 1838. [GM.ns10.566]

DOUGLAS, ROBERT, in Tobago, a deed, 1850. [NRS.RD5.842.62]

DOUGLAS, W. R. KEITH, a planter on Buccero Estate, Tobago, in 1836. [TNA.T47.1572]

DOUPNOY, JEAN, in St Vincent in 1777. [JCTP.84.69]

DOVALE, JOSIAU, died in Curacao on 1 February 1773, his widow SARA, died there on 8 March 1788. [Beth Hain Cemetery, Curacao]

DOWLAND, KAYE, a magistrate of the Leeward District, Tobago, in 1849. [TNA.CO390.4]

DOYLE, THOMAS WILLIAM, a printer and publisher, Long Lane, Rosseau, Dominica, 1859. [DC.954]

DRAGO, ABRAHAM, born 1628, a trader on Curacao from 1651-1655, later a merchant in Amsterdam trading with Curacao, died 1697.

DREW, JAMES, died in Tobago on 2 June 1798. [GM.68.811]

DRYSDALE, JAMES VICKERY, the Lieutenant Governor of Tobago from 1856 to 1865. [TNA.CO285.75]

DRYSDALE, ..., son of James S. Drysdale, was born in Castries, St Lucia, on 14 January 1839. [SG.8.768]

DU BOIS, CHARLES, in Dominica in 1776. [JCTP.83.35]

DU BOIS, JEAN PIERRE, in Grenada in 1769. [JCTP.1769.156]

DU CASSE, ..., in Martinique in 1707. [JCTP.1707.455]

DU FAIJ, ..., Governor of Curacao in 1720s

DUFF, DANIEL, born 1720, a labourer from Perthshire, banished to the Leeward Islands, liberated by the French and landed in Martinique in 1747. [TNA.SP36.102][P.2.168]

DUGUID, ALEXANDER, formerly in Grenada, later in Aberdeen, testament, 14 May 1800, Comm. Aberdeen. [NRS]

DU JARDAIN, PRILLEUX, in St Vincent in 1773. [JCTP.1773.334]

DUMAS, ST JOHN, constable in St Patrick's, Dominica, 1847. [DC.27.2.1847]

DU MAY, CLAUDE DUVAL, in St Vincent in 1771. [JCTP.1771.274]

DUNBAR, CHARLES, a merchant, died in Curacao in 1813. [GM.83.670]

DUNBAR, JAMES, born 1729, a labourer from Moray, a Jacobite banished to the Leeward Islands, liberated by the French and landed on Martinique in 1747. [TNA.SP36.102][P.2.170]

DUNBAR, ROBERT, born 1785, eldest son of William Dunbar in London, died in Dominica on 7 September 1804. [SM.66.973][GM.74.1168]

DUNBAR, THOMAS, a Major General in Tobago, died in Elgin, testament, 6 April 1818, Comm. Moray. [NRS]

DUNBAR, WILLIAM, born in Moy, Culbin, son of Reverend Robert Dunbar of Ballinspink, [1707-1782], and his wife Jean Miller, [died 1788], sometime in Grenada, later an attorney in London. [F.6.411]

DUNCAN, ADAM, assistant surgeon of the 67th Regiment, son of Alexander Duncan a merchant in Aberdeen, died in St Joseph's, Trinidad, on 7 October 1838. [AJ.4745]

DUNCAN, ALEXANDER, son of Alexander Duncan in Tobago, was educated at King's College, Aberdeen, in 1790. [KCA.2.371]

DUNCAN, JOHN, a merchant, youngest son of George Duncan the Controller of Stamp Duty in Scotland, died in Tobago on 30 March 1820. [S.4.201][AJ.3802]

DUNCAN, Dr THOMAS, in Grenada, 1804, [NRS.GD267.5.12] [NRAS.O682]; whose sons Thomas and Frank were educated at the Edinburgh Academy in the 1820s. [EAR]; from Grenada, died in Leathcote, West Lothian, on 17 June 1849. [SG.1831]

DUNCAN, Mrs, wife of Councillor Thomas Duncan, died in Grenada on 25 June 1818. [GM.88.373]

DUNCANSON, HUGH, born 1756, a carpenter from Scotland, emigrated via London aboard the Friendship bound for St Vincent in February 1774. [TNA.T47.9-11]

DUNLOP, WILLIAM, born 1775, fourth son of David Dunlop [1739-1804], a farmer in Loans, and his wife Agnes Dickie, [1752-1798], died in Grenada in 1790. [Dundonald gravestone]

DUNLOP, JAMES, a merchant from Garnkirk, died in Curacao, probate, 1684, PCC. [TNA]

DUNLOP, WILLIAM, born 1775, son of David Dunlop [1739-1804] and his wife Agnes Dickie [1742-1798], died in Grenada in 1790. [Dundonald gravestone]

DUNLOP, ..., son of Lieutenant Colonel Dunlop of the 2nd West Indian Regiment, was born in St James, Trinidad, on 15 November 1865. [GM.ns3/1.113]

DUNDON, PATRICK, in Martinique, probate, 1795, PCC. [TNA]

DU PARQUET, ..., Governor of Martinique in 1640. [SPAWI.1730.324]

DUPGUY, J. B., warden of St Mark's parish, Dominica, 1847. [DC27.2.1847]

DU PLESSIS, GOSELIN, in St Vincent in 1772. [JCTP.1772.319]

DURHAM, FRANCES ELIZA, only daughter of William Hall Durham a barrister in St Vincent, married W. Tawzia Savary, youngest son of Colonel W. J. T. Savary, in London in 1828. [GM.ns2/5.304]

DURHAM, WILLIAM HALL, a barrister in St Vincent, died in Kingston, St Vincent, on 3 November 1807. [GM.78.86]

THE PEOPLE OF THE WINDWARD ISLANDS, TRINIDAD AND TOBAGO, AND CURACAO, 1620-1860

DURIE, JOHN, born 1772, eldest son of Robert Durie in Glasgow, was educated at Glasgow University in 1788, died in Trinidad on 13 January 1811. [MAGU.154]

DU QUESNE, ..., Governor of Martinique in 1715-1716. [SPAWI.1715.244i/439/654iii/etc][JCTP.1716.206]

DUTTON, JOHN, born 1759, a clerk from London, emigrated via London aboard the Squirrel bound for the Grenades in December 1773. [TNA.T47.9-11]

DUVAL, ..., a planter, from London, emigrated aboard the Proudfoot bound via Plymouth for Grenada in October 1774. [TNA.T47.9/11]

DYCE, F. PETER, born 1773, MD, died in St Vincent on 26 January 1793. [AJ.2364]

DYKES, MARGARET, born 1725, from Linlithgow, a Jacobite banished to the Leeward Islands, liberated by the French and landed on Martinique in 1747. [TNA.SP36.102][P.2.170]

D'YLAN, JOAU DE DAVID, a rabbi on Curacao in 1674.

EAGLESHAM, HUGH, born 1839, youngest son of Hugh Eaglesham a dyer in Greenhead, Glasgow, died on 16 September 1859 in Port of Spain, Trinidad. [CM.21864]

ECCLES, GEORGE, a merchant in Trinidad, co-owner of the Commerce of Glasgow in 1798, and the Fame of Glasgow in 1802. [NRS.CE60.11.5/50; 7/13]

ECCLES, JAMES, a merchant in Trinidad, co-owner of the Commerce of Glasgow in 1798, and the Fame of Glasgow in 1802. [NRS.CE60.11.5/50; 7/13]

ECCLES, WILLIAM, born 1816, a Member of the Legislative Council, died in Enmore, Port of Spain, Trinidad, on 20 August 1859. [GM.ns2/7.430][CM.21834][EEC.23417]

ECCLES, ..., son of William Eccles, born 27 March 1854 in Port of Spain, Trinidad. [EEC.22574]

EDMONDS, JOHN, born 1762, a servant aboard the Le Soy Planter bound from London to Dominica in July 1774. [TNA.T9/11]

EDWARD, ANDREW, born 1722, a servant from Angus, a Jacobite banished to the Leeward Islands, liberated by the French and landed on Martinique in 1747. [TNA.SP36.102][P.2.176]

EDWARD, DAVID, [?], ['Davit Edwort'], a witness in Curacao on 20 August 1641. [NY Hist. ms, Dutch vol. ii, 1642-1647, Reg. of Prov. Sec.]

EDWARDS, WILLIAM, a merchant from Bristol, died in St Vincent in January 1810. [GM.80.384]

ELIGMEAR, FREDERICK, born 1750, a physician from London, emigrated via London aboard the Diana bound for Dominica in April 1774. [TNA.T47.9-11]

ELLIOT, AGNES MCRAE, only daughter of George Elliot of H.M.Commissariat Department, married Hew Manners Dalrymple of the 1st Regiment of Foot, in Tobago in August 1828. [BM.25.816]

ELLIOT, JANE, from Tobago, died in Glasgow on 13 February 1851. [W.1192]

ELLIS, JAN, a planter at Savonet, Curacao, in 1719

ELLIS, JAN, born in St Eustatia, a Dutch Reformed Church minister in Willemstad, Curacao, from 1751 until 1771. [NAN.OAC.1.05.12.1/204]

ELWIN, H. S., born 1820, eldest son of Reverend T. H. Elwin in East Hertfordshire, died in Boteau, Dominica, on 1 June 1838. [GM.ns10.342]

EMES, THOMAS, Lieutenant Colonel of the 5th Regiment, born 1769, died in Dominica on 2 November 1824. [St George church, Roseau]

ESDRE, GODFRIED C., settled in Curacao in 1731

EWING, GEORGE, born 1754, a carpenter from Edinburgh, from London aboard the Greyhound bound for Dominica in December 1773. [TNA.T47.9-11]

EWING, ROBERT, born 5 March 1786, only son of Walter Ewing jr. a merchant in Glasgow, died in Trinidad on 6 June 1801. [GM.72.781][AJ.2848]

FABER, FREDERICK, born 1750, a merchant in London, emigrated via London aboard the Simond bound for the Grenades in December 1773. [TNA.T47.9-11]

FADELLE, JOSEPH, Speaker of the House of Assembly of Dominica in 1840. [DC:1.8.1840]

FAESCH, ISAAC, Governor of Curacao from 1740 to 1758. [NWIC.585/49]

FAGAN, JAMES, in Grenada, probate, 1802, PCC. [TNA]

FAIRBAIRN, JOHN, manager of Waltham Estate, Grenada, in 1812. [NRS.NRAS.00682; GD267.5.24]

FAIRBAIRN, THOMAS, in St Vincent, nephew of Reverend Thomas Fairbairn in Gartly, a sasine, 8 April 1793. [NRS.RS.Aberdeen. 1172]

FAIRHOLM, ADAM, in Tobago, probate 1772, PCC. [TNA]

FAIRHOLM, THOMAS, a merchant from Edinburgh, in Tobago, in 1779. [NRS.CS16.1.175]

FAIRLEY, EDWARD, born 1825, second son of Edward Fairley of the Royal Bank in Glasgow, died in Port of Spain, Trinidad, on 24 February 1846. [AJ.5218]

FALCONER, ARCHIBALD, a merchant in Trinidad, married Mary Anne Porter, daughter of Matthew Porter an accountant in Glasgow, there on 12 September 1837. [DPCA.1834]

FALCONER, COLIN, an indentured servant from Edinburgh, on Ninian Home's plantation in Grenada in 1794. [NRS.GD267.5.32]

FALCONER, ROBERT, born 1821, youngest son of Mr Falconer in Silverhills, died in Trinidad on 4 May 1838. [AJ.4770]

FALCONER, WILLIAM, born 1807, son of Captain D. Falconer and his wife Catherine, died in Grenada on 30 May 1844. [Rothes gravestone]

FALL, RICHARD, married Eliza Whiteman, daughter of Andrew Whiteman, in Grenada on 17 June 1820. [GM.90.636]

FALSIDE, MARGARET ANNE, daughter of Dr Falside in St Vincent, married John Carmichael, a Lieutenant of the 53rd Regiment, in St Vincent on 24 August 1797. [GM.67.1127][EEC.420.97]

FALSIDE, WILLIAM, a surgeon, died in Dominica on 6 March 1813. [EA.5156.13]; [NRS.RD5.159.216]

FARQUHAR, ANDREW, in Grenada, was granted the lands of Auchintoul on 3 February 1800. [NRS.RGS.131.93]

FARQUHARSON, Major General JAMES ALEXANDER, of Oakley, Governor General of St Lucia, died there on 23 January 1834. [SG.3.232][GM.104.317]

FARQUHARSON, JOHN, in Grenada in 1792. [NRS.NRAS.61.2.2]; in Grenada, probate, 1801, PCC. [TNA]

FELICIEN, Father, a French Catholic priest in Grenada in 1793. [FPA.291]

FENWICK, GEORGE, son of George Fenwick a goldsmith in Edinburgh, died in Castara, Tobago, on 4 September 1821. [S.5.252]

FENWICK, JAMES, Customs Controller of St Vincent, died 1777. [GM.48.391]

FERGERSON, FAUDE, born 1706, died in Trinidad on 15 June 1836. [GM.ns6.223]

FERGUSON, DUNCAN, in St Lucia, a deed, 1836. [NRS.RD5.544.557]

FERGUSON, JAMES, son of Sir James Ferguson, died in Tobago in 1777. [GM.48.45]; youngest brother of Sir Adam Ferguson of Kilkerran, died in Tobago in 1778. [Ruddiman's Weekly Mercury.iv]

FERGUSON, JAMES, born 1813, a merchant from Edinburgh, died in Trinidad on 7 July 1868. [St Cuthbert's gravestone, Edinburgh]

FERGUSON, JOHN, born 1784, died in Charlottetown, Grenada, on 21 November 1868. [S.7918]

FERGUSON, ROBERT, late in Grenada, testament, 1793, Comm. Edinburgh. [NRS]

FERGUSON, ..., son of Alvin P. Ferguson, was born in Charlottetown, Grenada, on 4 July 1868. [S.7800]

FERRIER, WILLIAM, a mason in Grenada in 1805, later in Glasgow in 1810. [NRS.RS.Glasgow.5624; SC58.59.7.55]; a deed, 6 December 1827. [NRS.RD5.369.186]

FILLAN, C. A., Clerk of the Assembly of Dominica in 1840. [DC:1.8.1840]

THE PEOPLE OF THE WINDWARD ISLANDS, TRINIDAD AND TOBAGO, AND CURACAO, 1620-1860

FINDLATOR, JOHN, a minister sent to the Grenades in 1771. [EMA.27]; in St Vincent in 1796. [FPA.292]; died in London in 1809. [GM.79.1238]

FINDLAY, JAMES, a printer, died in Grenada in 1800. [AJ.2749]

FINLAY, JOHN, warden of St Patrick's parish, Dominica, 1847. [DC27.2.1847]

FINLAY, Mrs, a lady from London, from Portsmouth aboard the Grenville Bay from Portsmouth bound for Grenada in December 1775. [TNA.T47.9/11]

FISHER, BENJAMIN, an engineer from London, emigrated via Plymouth aboard the Lovely Betsy bound for Dominica in March 1774. [TNA.T47.9-11]

FITZWILLIAM, GEORGE, a shipping agent on King's Wharf, Port of Spain, Trinidad, 1843. [PSG.1806]

FLANDRIN, JOHN CHARLES, in Grenada in 1769. [JCTP.1769.156]

FLEMING, DAVID, in Trinidad, 1846. [TS:1.1.1846]

FLEMING, J. R., an auctioneer in San Fernando, Trinidad, in 1843. [PSG.1806]

FLOWERS, ..., an officer of H.M. Ordnance, via Portsmouth aboard the Grenville Bay bound for Grenada in December 1775. [TNA.T47.9/11]

FORBES, DAVID, born 1801, eldest son of Alexander Forbes in New Laverockbank, died in Tobago on 21 September 1831. [EEC.18730[

FORBES, DUNCAN, in Tobago and Grenada, died in Grenada on 10 November 1791, probate 1792 PCC. [TNA] [GC.63][GM.62.88]

FORBES, EUPHEMIA, eldest daughter of Patrick Forbes in Grenada, died in Glasgow on 16 February 1806. [GM.76.284]

FORBES, GEORGE, a planter, died in Tobago on 30 August 1786. [GM.57.89]

FORBES, GEORGE, died 1802 in Grenada. [NRS.NRAS.3626.757]

FORBES, HARRY, born 1769, late of Grenada, died in Dee Street, Aberdeen, on 1 March 1843. [AJ.4965]

FORBES, HUGH, in St Vincent, probate, 1796, PCC. [TNA]

FORBES, PATRICK, only son of Patrick Forbes, a merchant in Grenada, matriculated at Glasgow University in 1811. [MAGU.260]

FORBES, THOMAS GRANVILLE, second son of Dr Forbes in Sutherland, died in St Vincent in 1825. [AJ.4022]

FORBES, WILLIAM, born 1745, a planter, from Plymouth to Tobago aboard the London in January 1775. [TNA.T47.9-11]; possibly died on the Culloden Estate there in 1806. [AJ.3055]

FORBES, WILLIAM, in Vengeance, Prince Rupert Bay, Dominica, in 1798, nephew of William Forbes of Callander. [NRS.RH1.2.808]

FORBES-LEITH, RALPH, MD, son of George Forbes-Leith of Knock, Aberdeenshire, died in Carriacou on 22 August 1868. [AJ.4.11.1868]

FORSTER, MATTHEW FREDERICK, Captain of the 4th West Indian Regiment, died in St George, Grenada, on 7 May 1796. [GM.66.701]

FORSYTH, WILLIAM, born 1817, SON OF Robert Forsyth a farmer in Keith, Banffshire, died in Trinidad on 4 December 1850. [W.1185] [EEC.22071]

FORSYTH, WILLIAM, from Huntly, Aberdeenshire, died in Trinidad on 4 January 1851. [AJ.5374]

FORTHTON, JAMES, born in Bordeaux in 1645, settled in the West Indies in 1694, married in St Kitts, resided in Martinique for 30 years, in Grenada for 40 years, died there in 1773. [GM.43.154]

FORTUNE, ALEXANDER, son of Dr John Fortune in Grenada, died in Melbourne on 28 January 1854. [FH.20.4.1854]

THE PEOPLE OF THE WINDWARD ISLANDS, TRINIDAD AND TOBAGO, AND CURACAO, 1620-1860

FORTUNE, JOHN, in Grenada in 1848. [NRS.RD5.819.581]

FOUKET, ..., born 1744, a planter, from London to Grenada aboard the Mary in February 1774. [TNA.T47.9-11]

FOURNIER, PROSPER, in Grenada in 1769. [JCTP.1769.156]

FRASER, ALEXANDER, second son of James Fraser of Belladrum, a merchant in Tobago, died in 1784, a will. [NRS.GD23.10.594]

FRASER, CHARLES SHULDHAM, born 1783, a magistrate of St George, Grenada, died there on 4 October 1850. [GM.NS34.678] [AJ.5367]

FRASER, ELIZABETH BRISTOW, relict of Richard Landreth of Grenada, died 32 Alva Street, Edinburgh, on 5 July 1848. [EEC.21676]

FRASER, GEORGE, born 2 July 1767 in Moneydie, Perthshire, son of Reverend George Fraser and his wife Agnes Thomson, died in Grenada on 17 August 1795. [F.4.225]

FRASER, GEORGE, born 1804, second son of Angus Fraser and his wife Elizabeth Sutherland in Dornoch, married Emily Kerr, second daughter of John Charles Kerr of Beaumont Lodge, in St George's, Grenada, on 28 April 1838, parents of John, Angus, William and Franklyn, George died in 1855. [AJ.4722]

FRASER, JAMES, youngest son of William Fraser a coach proprietor in Edinburgh, died in Dominica on 29 July 1867. [S.7511]

FRASER, Mrs JANE, widow of Alexander Fraser in Dominica, died at 6 Nelson Street, Edinburgh, on 29 February 1848. [EEC.21625]

FRASER, JOHN, a planter in Dominica from 1800 until his death in 1803, son of William Fraser of Culbokie. [AJ.2934][NRS.AD58.263]

FRASER, LIONEL, a Lieutenant of the 41st Regiment, married Louise Amenaiche Guiseppe, second daughter of Jose Guiseppe the Consul to

Venezuela, in Port of Spain, Trinidad, on 21 November 1857. [GM.ns2/4.207]

FRASER, LOUISA AMENAIDE, wife of Lionel Mordaunt Fraser the Registrar of the Supreme Court of Trinidad, died in Port of Spain, Trinidad, on 1 July 1879. [EC.29602]

FRASER, SIMON, jr., only son of S. Fraser in London, died in Dominica on 6 August 1793, [GM.63.958]; probate 1794, PCC. [TNA]

FRASER, SIMON, in Dominica, probate, 1803, PCC. [TNA]

FRASER, WILLIAM, a planter in St Vincent, probate, 1802, PCC. [TNA]

FRASER, WILLIAM, in Willytone, St Vincent, in 1803, only son of Hugh Fraser a tenant in Kiltarlity, Inverness. [NRS.GD128.52.5]

FRASER, ..., son of George Fraser, was born on 6 February 1841 at Mount Parnassus, Grenada. [AJ.4865]

FRASER, ..., warden of St David's parish, Dominica, 1847. [DC27.2.1847]

FRASER, ..., son of Andrew Fraser, was born in Grenada on 18 December 1876. [EC.28827]

FRENCH, ADELAIDE AMELIA LESLIE, daughter of George Henry French, of Richmond Hill, St Vincent, married John Hewetson of London, in Hampstead on 15 March 1859. [GM.ns2/6.424]

FRENCH, JAMES BOGLE, in Grenada, probate 1792, PCC. [TNA]

FRENCH, JAMES CHARLES, born 1793, a Counsellor of St Vincent, died 14 February 1832. [St Vincent gravestone]

FREW, SOPHIA LOUISA, infant daughter of Reverend J. M. Frew, Rector of St Thomas in the East, Jamaica, died in Grenada on 24 February 1842. [GSP.718]

FRITH, THOMAS, born 1754, a gentleman, from London to Grenada aboard the Mary in February 1774. [TNA.T47.9-11]

FULLARTON, DAVID, a minister sent to Dominica in 1767. [FPA.327][EMA.28]

FULLER, HENRY, born 1781, Attorney General, died at The Rookery, Maraval, Trinidad, on 23 September 1854. [GM.ns42.638]

FYFE, LAWRENCE, son of MacDuff Fiyfe in St Vincent, was educated at King's College, Aberdeen, 1819-1820. [KCA.2.438]

FYFE, MACDUFF, son of John Fyffe in Cabrach, was educated at King's College, Aberdeen, from 1785 to 1789, later a planter in St Vincent. [KCA.2.364]

GACHETTE, GEORGE, constable in St Mark's, Dominica, in 1847. [DC.27.2.1847]

GAHAGAN, JAMES, in Grenada, probate, 1807, PCC. [TNA]

GAIRDNER, ALEXANDER, Fourth son of Alexander Gairdner in Ayr, a planter on Adelphi Estate, Tobago, in 1836. [TNA.T71.1572]; died there on 18 January 1849. [NRS.GD1.380.52][EEC.21781]; a judge and councillor, died in Tobago in December 1848. [GM.ns31.446]

GALE, JAN, probably from Frisia, Governor of Curacao from 1738 to 1740. [NWIC.580.36/229; 582.610; 583.229]

GALLAGHER, MARTIN, a printer and publisher of the 'Trinidad Gazette', died in Trinidad on 21 October 1819. [GM.89.278]

GALLIE, ..., son of William Holmes Gallie, was born in Port of Spain, Trinidad, on 15 May 1863, another son was born there on 28 May 1868. [S.7919/7774]

GARDEN, ALEXANDER, in Tobago in 1778, brother of Charles Garden a writer in Edinburgh. [NRS.CS16.1.174]

GARDINER, ELIZABETH, daughter of David Gardiner of Kirktonhill, married William Richardson, in St Vincent on 7 October 1789. [GM.59.954]

GARDNER, GORDON, son of Edwin Gardner in Trinidad, was educated at King's College, Aberdeen, from 1817 to 1818. [KCA]

GARDNER, STEPHEN GIBSON, eldest son of an apothecary in Edinburgh, died in Trinidad in 1817. [S.i.31]

GARDNER, WILLIAM, son of Edwin Gardner in Trinidad, was educated at King's College, Aberdeen, in 1817. [KCA.2.432]

GARNETT, Reverend James, BA of Trinity College, Cambridge, son of Reverend W. Garnett in Barbados, died in Scarborough, Tobago, on 4 January 1842. [GM.ns17.557]

GARNIER, WILLIAM, in Dominica in 1772. [JCTP.79]

GARRANEY, HENRY, born 1806, died in Observatory Cottage, Grenada, on 17 September 1868. [SG.7879]

GARRAWAY, FREDERICK HERVEY, born 1791, from Dominica, died in London on 3 July 1856. [GM.ns2/1.260]

GARRAWAY, JOHN, in Grenada, probate, 1810, PCC. [TNA]

GAVIN, THOMAS, a merchant in Grenada in 1809. [GA.T-ARD.13,1]

GAYRIN, ALEXIS, in St Vincent in 1773. [JCTP.1773.334]

GAYRIN, PIERRE, in St Vincent in 1773. [JCTP.1773.334]

GEDDES, WILLIAM, born 1848, son of James Geddes a clogger in Lochmaben, Dumfries-shire, a plantation overseer in Tobago, died there on 14 August 1870. [AO]

GELLION, ARTHUR GEORGE, born 1819, son of Thomas Gellion [1781-1840] and his wife Helen McKinnon [1782-1829], died in Dominica on 25 April 1858. [Inverness Chapelyard gravestone]

GEROLD and URICH, in King Street, Port of Spain, Trinidad, 1843. [PSG.1806]

GIBBS, DANIEL, in Grenada, 1809, see Dr David Linton's testament.; born 1781, settled in Grenada before 1797, a Councillor, died in Grenada on 29 December 1837. [GM.ns9.447]

GIBBS, DAVID, in Grenada, 1809, see Dr David Linton's testament.

GIBBS, DAVID WILLIAM, born 1815, agent for the Royal Mail Steam Packet Company, died in Grenada on 28 June 1868. [S.7800]

GIBBS, EDWARD, born 1791, from Brixton, Surrey, died in Grenada on 31 August 1855. [GM.ns54.553]

GIBBES, SAMUEL OSBORNE, youngest son of Sir Philip Gibbes, HM Receiver in Grenada, died there in January 1807. [GM.77.376]

GIBBS, SARAH, born 1796, wife of E. Gibbs of London and Grenada, died in London on 12 July 1831. [GM.101.91]

GIBBS, Mrs, formerly Bishop from Exeter, wife of Samuel Osborn Gibbs, died in Grenada on 20 August 1804. [GM.74.1071]

GIBBONS, THOMAS, in Tobago, died 1773. [GM.43.154]

GIBSON, MANIE, daughter of Robert Gibson a merchant in Tobago, married John Shaw, a surgeon in Edinburgh, there on 27 August 1787. [EMR]

GIBSON, SARAH, born 10 March 1807, daughter of James Gibson and his wife Mary Wilson in Dollar, died in Tobago on 9 June 1902. [Dollar gravestone]

GIFFORD, PAUL, a merchant in Bridge Street, Castries, St Lucia, 1859. [DC:954]

GILBERT, JOHN D., fifth son of Captain William Gilbert of the 52nd Foot, died on Bon Air estate, Trinidad, on 10 July 1848. [SG.1744]

GILDING, Reverend JOHN, Rector of St George and St Andrew in St Vincent, died 25 July 1818. [St Vincent gravestone]

GILDING, MARY, wife of Reverend Lansdown Gilding, died 15 November 1827. [St Vincent gravestone]

GILLAN, JOHN, a merchant planter in Dominica in 1776. [NRS.NRAS.0631.GDB3]

GILLAN, JOHN, warden of St Andrew's parish, Dominica, in 1847. [DC27.2.1847]

GILLEBER, ..., in Curacao, a letter, 1709. [SPAWI.1709.411i]

GILLESPIE, JOHN, born 23 November 1797 in Arrocher, Dunbartonshire, son of Reverend John Gillespie and his wife Bethia Erskine, died in St Vincent on 24 September 1833. [F.3.326]

GILLOCK, JAMES, the Registrar of Grenada in 1772. [NRS.RD2.224/2.650]

GILLON, JOHN, born 1749 in London, late in Dominica, died in London on 14 January 1810. [GM.80.89]; a merchant planter in Dominica in 1776, [NRS.NRAS.0631, GDB.3]; late in Dominica, was granted Wellhouse on 20 December 1805. [RGS.135/169/240]; in Dominica, probate, 1810, PCC. [TNA]

GILMORE, JOSEPH DENT, an Anglican minister, sent to Grenada in 1801. [EMA.30]

GILSMAN, Miss, died in Tobago on 8 April 1811. [GM.81.88]

GIRAULT, JEAN BAPTISTE, in Dominica in 1772. [JCTP.1772.319]

GIUSEPPI, MATTHEW, a surgeon in London and Trinidad, died 13 January 1846. [GM.ns25.219]

GLANVILLE, JOSEPH W., a barrister in Dominica, died on 8 February 1847. [DC27.2.1847]

GLASFORD, ROBERT, from Glasgow, a merchant in Grenada, co-owner of the Montreal Plantation, Grenada, deed, 17 January 1764. [GA.T-MJ]

GLASGOW, ROBERT, a planter of Mount Greenan, St Vincent, from 1784 to 1831, a deed, 16 May 1795, [NRS.RD3.300.272]; later in Mount Greenan, Irvine, Ayrshire, in 1821. [NRS.CS17.1.40.274; GD1.584.1]

GLEAN, JAMES, born 1814, a colonial officer, died in Charlottetown, Grenada, on 10 August 1867. [S.75281]

GLEDSTANE, JOHN, in Trinidad, probate, 1808, PCC. [TNA]

GLENNY, ALEXANDER, in Dominica, probate, 1787, PCC. [TNA]

GLOSTER, ARCHIBALD, the Attorney General of Trinidad, married Miss Thompson from Tooting, Surrey, on 22 October 1806. [GM.76.978]

GLOSTER, SARAH, born 1786, widow of Archibald Gloster the Chief Justice of Dominica, died in Nantes on 15 December 1855. [GM.ns43.327]

GLOSTER, WILLIAM JARVIS, son of Archibald Gloster the Attorney General of Trinidad, died in London on 22 September 1806. [GM.76.984]

GLUYAS, WILLIAM, warden of St Paul's parish, Dominica, in 1847. [DC27.2.1847]

GODART, MARMADUKE, in St Lucia in 1730. [SPAWI.1730.260.v/vi]

GOLLAN, GILBERT, late of St Vincent, probate, 1809, PCC. [TNA]; 1821. [NRS.CS17.1.40/198]; his widow Isabel, in St Vincent, 1813, [NRS.CS96.3571/3]; a sasine, 1819. [NRS.RS.Inverness.1874]

GOMEZ, ANTONIO, a former Councillor of Trinidad, died in Philadelphia on 20 June 1843. [GM.ns20.334]

GOMEZ, PHILIP, the Registrar of Trinidad, eldest son of Antonio Gomez a judge in Trinidad, died in Port of Spain, Trinidad, on 23 July 1866. [GM.ns3/2.695]

GOODBRAND, ALEXANDER, born 1716, a carpenter from Banff, a Jacobite banished to the Leeward Islands, liberated by the French and landed on Martinique in 1747. [TNA.SP36.102][P.2.248]

GORDON, ADAM, born 11 October 1812, son of Reverend William Gordon and his wife Catherine Brodie, in Elgin, Moray, died on Richmond Estate, St Vincent, on 23 March 1832. [F.6.391][AJ.4401][EEC.18803]

GORDON, ALEXANDER NATHANIEL, son of Alexander Gordon [1682-1748], a farmer in Kirkcowan, Wigtownshire, a merchant in Glasgow and a land-owner in St John's, Tobago, 1770. ['Hooper's Account of Tobago, London, 1777]

GORDON, ALEXANDER, born 1755, son of Reverend Harry Gordon, [1730-1764], and his wife Sarabella Morrison in Fordyce, Banffshire, a planter in Tobago, died 1781. [F.5.434]

GORDON, ALEXANDER, in Belmont, Tobago, a sasine, 1786, [NRS.RS38.15.15]; was granted the lands of Pitlurg on 5 July 1794. [NRS.RGS.127.158]; in Tobago in 1800. [NRS.GD44.34.48.2]; younger brother of Baron Gordon of the Exchequer in Scotland, died in Bath on 11 January 1801. [GM.71.92]; probate, 1801, PCC. [TNA]

GORDON, ALEXANDER, of Grafton Plantation, St Patrick's parish, Tobago, husband of Jane Margaret Morison, daughter of Alexander Morison of Bogrie, relict of James Ogilvie of Ascruives, in 1794. [NRS.NRAS.297.120]

GORDON, ALEXANDER, of Cluny, a planter on Bacelot Estate, Tobago, in 1836. [TNA.T47.1572]

GORDON, ANTHONY, a planter in Dominica, a deed in 1772. [NRS.RD3.231.898]

GORDON, BENJAMIN, in Dominica, probate 1783, PCC. [TNA]

GORDON, ELIZABETH, youngest daughter of William Gordon of Banff, Scotland, and Dominica, married James Rae of the Royal Navy, in St Luke's, Chelsea, on 5 December 1827. [EA.6683.799]

GORDON, ELIZABETH, youngest daughter of William Gordon of Banff, Scotland, and Dominica, married James Rae of the Royal Navy, in St Luke's, Chelsea, on 5 December 1827. [EA.6683.799]

GORDON, HUGH, from Dominica, married Catherine Wilson in Macduff, Banffshire, on 27 October 1807. [DPCA]

GORDON, JAMES, late of Tobago, died in Tillynaught on 15 April 1793. [AJ.2364]

GORDON, JAMES, of Tobago, died in London on 23 March 1806, [GM.76.385]; probate, 1806, PCC. [TNA]

GORDON, JOHN, born 1728, a weaver from Elgin, a Jacobite banished to the Leeward Islands, liberated by the French and landed on Martinique in 1747. [TNA.SP36.102][P.2.238]

GORDON, JOHN, in Bellmont, Tobago, a sasine, 29 September 1786. [NRS.RS.Aberdeen.512]

THE PEOPLE OF THE WINDWARD ISLANDS, TRINIDAD AND TOBAGO, AND CURACAO, 1620-1860

GORDON, JOHN, a carpenter in Tobago in 1800. [NRS.GD44.34.46.2]

GORDON, JOHN, of Cluny, a planter on Bacelot Estate, Tobago, in 1836. [TNA.T47.1572]

GORDON, JOHN, of Newton, a planter on Grafton and Grange Estates, Tobago, in 1836. [TNA.T71.1572]

GORDON, J.B., in Grenada, an entail, 20 December 1769. [NRS.RD4.208.1380]

GORDON, MARY, born 1764, widow of William Gordon of Banff [GM.ns42.314]

GORDON, PETER, in Grenada, was 'killed by Mr Proudfoot in a duel' in 1768. [GM.38.446]

GORDON, Colonel ROBERT, born 1740, President of St Vincent, died there on 16 September 1829/1830 {?]. [GM.100.381][AJ.4275]

GORDON, ROBERT, in St Vincent in 1797. [see Duncan Campbell's will, probate 6 October 1797, PCC.TNA]

GORDON, WILLIAM, late of Tobago, 1816. [NRS.GD74.163]

GORDON, WILLIAM, born 1780, a planter in Tobago, died in West Lodge, Elgin, Morayshire, on 29 November 1831. [Rothes Dundorcas gravestone][AJ.4378][SNQ.IX.157]

GORDON, Mrs, wife of Captain Gordon the Quarter-master of Trinidad, died there on 13 September 1817. [GM.87.561]

GORRIE, Sir JOHN, born 1829, son of Reverend Daniel Gorrie, Chief Justice of Tobago from1886 to 1888, Chief Justice of Trinidad and Tobago from 1889 until his death in 1892.

GRAEME, FRANCES SARAH, eldest daughter of Major Lawrence Graeme the Lieutenant Governor of Tobago, married John Paul

Thornton, the Colonial Secretary, third son of Thomas Thornton in Constantinople, in Tobago on 25 May 1846. [GM.ns26.196]

GRAEME, Major LAWRENCE, Lieutenant Governor of Jamaica, born 1796, third son of Colonel Graeme of Inchbrakie, Perthshire, died at Government House, Tobago, on 14 December 1850. [W.1191]

GRAHAM, JAMES, of Dougaldston, then in Grenada in 1776. [NLS.Acc.8793]; 1778, [NRS.CS16.1.173.157]

GRAHAM, JAMES, a merchant in Glasgow, partner in the firm Graham and Neilson, died in Trinidad, testament, 11 July 1806, Comm. Glasgow. [NRS]

GRAHAM, JOHN, from Dougaldston, Scotland, later in Dougaldston, Grenada, son of Janet Luke, 1771. [GA.623/T-MJ76]

GRAHAM, JOHN, in Grenada in 1776. [NLS.Acc.8793.6]

GRAHAM, ROBERT, an estate overseer in Dominica, died November 1780, testament, 1808, Comm. Edinburgh. [NRS.GD22.2.67]

GRAHAM, ROBERT, a planter and overseer in Dominica, died 26 June 1783. [EA][NRS.GD22.2.67]

GRAHAM, WILLIAM, a merchant, married Jessie youngest daughter of John Taylor jr., a merchant in Glasgow, in San Fernando, Trinidad, on 24 October 1849. [SG.18.1878]

GRAHAM, WILLIAM MARTIN, born 1827, eldest son of Joseph Graham in Port of Spain, Trinidad, died in Stonehouse in January 1845. [GM.ns23.216]

GRAHAM, ..., daughter of Cyril Clark Graham, was born in Government House, Grenada, on 9 December 1875. [EC.28502]

THE PEOPLE OF THE WINDWARD ISLANDS, TRINIDAD AND TOBAGO, AND CURACAO, 1620-1860

GRANNUM, HENRY, died at Mount Gay, St Lucia, on 21 August 1854. [TNA.CO.33.12]

GRANT, ALEXANDER, born 1722, a carpenter from Aberdeen, a Jacobite banished to the Leeward Islands, liberated by the French and landed on Martinique in 1747. [TNA.SP36.102][P.2.250]

GRANT, ANDREW, in Grenada in 1779. [NRS.CS16.1.175]; died in Grenada in 1780. [GM.50.153]; probate, 1783, PCC. [TNA]

GRANT, BARBARA MARY, youngest daughter of G. Colquhoun Grant the Treasurer of St Vincent, married Dawson Stockley Warren a Captain of the 14th Regiment, on Morne Estate, St Lucia, on 24 February 1863. [GM.ns2/14.515]

GRANT, CAROLINE MAYER, second daughter of George Colquhoun Grant, married Reverend Alexander Dasent, fourth son of J. R. Dasent, the Attorney General of St Vincent, there on 13 October 1847. [GM.ns29.80]

GRANT, CHARLES, born 1728, a miller from Abernethy, a Jacobite banished to the Leeward Islands, liberated by the French and landed on Martinique in 1747. [TNA.SP36.102][P.2.252]

GRANT, CHARLES, a merchant in St Vincent, a deed, 26 January 1796. [Caribeanna.3.27]

GRANT, CHARLOTTE, born 1791, widow of Charles Grant in Trinidad and Martinique, died in Dawlish on 27 December 1859. [GM.ns2/8.198]

GRANT, HENRIETTA, daughter of Andrew Grant in London and Grenada, died in Clifton, Gloucestershire, on 30 September 1840. [GM.ns14.672]

THE PEOPLE OF THE WINDWARD ISLANDS, TRINIDAD AND TOBAGO, AND CURACAO, 1620-1860

GRANT, JAMES, born 1773, from St Vincent, died in London on 5 June 1837. [GM.ns8.99]

GRANT, JAMES MAYER, the Colonial Treasurer, married Marion, eldest daughter of Thomas Campbell of 21 George Square, Edinburgh, in Calligua, St Vincent, on 20 June 1855. [EEC.22768]

GRANT, Major General JERVIS, KCH, Governor of Trinidad, married Isabella Eleanora Grant, daughter of Alexander Grant of Tullochgrittan, in Trinidad on 31 July 1842. [CM.17342]

GRANT, JOHN, born 1707, a labourer from Badenoch or Lochaber, a Jacobite banished to the Leeward Islands, liberated by the French and landed on Martinique in 1747. [TNA.SP36.102][P.2.260]

GRANT, JOHN, of Braggan, a planter in Grenada, dead by 1750. [Aberdeen Sheriff Court, warrants, 15.2.1771]

GRANT, JOHN, born 1778, from Wallebow, St Vincent, died in London on 3 March 1820. [GM.90.284][AJ.3767]

GRANT, JOHN, from St Vincent, married Margaret Grant, eldest daughter of John Grant a solicitor in Keith, Banffshire, in London on 29 November 1849. [AJ.5217]

GRANT, Major General Sir LEWIS, Governor of Trinidad, married Isabella Elizabeth Grant, only daughter of A. Grant of Tullochgrigan, in Trinidad on 31 July 1832. [GM.102.263]

GRANT, ROBERT, in St Vincent, probate, 1803, PCC. [TNA]

GRANT, THOMAS, in St Vincent, [NRS.PS3.11.307]

GRANT, VIRGINIA, wife of James Meyer Grant, died in St Lucia on 12 January 1868. [GM.ns3/5.396]

GRANT, WILLIAM, born 1748, a gentleman aboard the Earl of Errol bound from Plymouth to the Grenades in March 1776. [TNA.T47.9-11]

GRANT, WILLIAM, of Glenbeg, a merchant and planter in Grenada, father of Charles Grant, 1778. [NRS.CS16.1.174]

GRANT, WILLIAM GORDON MACGREGOR, born 3 April 1801 in Grantown-on-Spey, a planter in St Vincent, died in Edinburgh on 15 September 1849. [Dean gravestone]

GRANT, ……, born 1735, a planter, with his wife born 1739, and three servants, bound from Plymouth to Grenada aboard the Laurent in January 1775. [TNA.T47.9-11]

GRAY, ALEXANDER, a merchant, married Captain Webster, paymaster of the 1st West India Regiment, in Trinidad on 8 June 1833. [SG.177]

GRAY, ALEXANDER, of Garden Estate, Trinidad, died in London on 20 August 1860. [EEC.23529]

GRAY, Dr ANDREW, died at Prince Rupert's Bay, Dominica, in September 1787. [SM]

GRAY, CHARLES, born 1766, of Observatory and Charlotteville, a Member of the Council and Colonel of Militia, died in Tobago on 15 September 1826. [AJ.4117]

GRAY, CHARLES, a planter on Highlands Estate, Tobago, in 1836. [TNA.T71.1572]

GRAY, JOSEPH, in Dominica, see deed dated 1 January 1785. [NRS.RD2.242.1.103]

GREAUX, JACQUES, in St Vincent in 1773. [JCTP.1773.334]

THE PEOPLE OF THE WINDWARD ISLANDS, TRINIDAD AND TOBAGO, AND CURACAO, 1620-1860

GREEN, ALEXANDER, born 1826, son of Peter Green and his wife Jane Horne, died in Tobago on 2 October 1847. [Holy Rude gravestone, Stirling]

GREENLEES, WILLIAM, a student, son of Matthew Greenlees a merchant in Campbelltown, died in Trinidad on 3 May 1842. [SG.11.1093]

GREENWAY, Dr JOHN, born 1759, settled in Dominica in 1788, died in Rosseau, Dominica, on 11 December 1828. [GM.99.190]

GREENWAY, Mrs MARGARET, third daughter of David Wardrobe a surgeon in Edinburgh, and wife of John Greenway of the Belfast Plantation, died in Roseau, Dominica, on 6 May 1811. [SM.73.637]

GREG, JOHN, in Dominica in 1771. [JCTP.78.186]; died 10 June 1795, his wife Catherine, born 1737, died 22 November 1819. [Hampton, Middlesex, gravestone][GM.478]

GREGORIE, CATHERINE, born 1794, widow of James Morris Collier in Tobago, died in London on 6 October 1853. [GM.ns40.650]

GREIG, Dr ANDREW, died at Prince Rupert's Bay, Dominica, in September 1787. [SM.49.621]

GREIG, Miss, daughter of W. Greig in St Vincent, married Lieutenant Colonel White of the 80th Regiment in 1810. [GM.80.383]

GRIMON, Father MIGUEL, an Augustinian priest, to Curacao in 1752, died in 1755.

GROVES, THOMAS, son of John Groves in London, died in Grenada in 1796. [GM.66.969]

GUILD, Dr GEORGE, in Tobago, died on passage to Baltimore on 30 September 1801. [GM.71.1211]

GUILDING, CLARISSA ELIZABETH, third daughter of Reverend Landsdown Guilding in St Vincent, married Denzil Holt Ibbotson, third son of Denzil Ibbetson, the Deputy Commissary General of Malta, in Bromley, Kent, on 28 May 1846. [GM.ns26.197]

GUISEPPI, JOSEPH ANTON, a stipendiary judge in Trinidad, 1846. [TS:1.1.1846]

GURLEY......., son of William Gurley of Peter's Hope, St Vincent, was born in Scarborough on 3 April 1825. [BM.17.759]

GURLEY, WILLIAM, of Petershope, St Vincent, Captain of the 55th [Aberdeenshire] Militia, was killed in a duel with Mr Westall, an English gentleman, in Queensferry, West Lothian, on 30 October 1824. [FH.4.11.1824]

GURLEY, Mrs, widow of Peter Gurley in St Vincent, daughter of Sir William Johnston of Custobers in Scotland, died in Needham Market on 23 March 1819. [GM.88.378]

GUTHRIE, JOHN, in Grenada, 1795, [NRS.GD18.275]; co-owner of the Pomona of Glasgow and of the Alfred of Glasgow in 1798. [NRS.CE60.11.5/71/108]

GWYER, MATTHEW WRIGHT, third son of William O. Gwyer in Bristol, died in St Vincent on 26 March 1842. [GM.ns18.335]

HACKSHAW, HARRY, born 1777, died 17 March 1845. [St Vincent gravestone]

HADDOW, JAMES, from London, died in Grenada on 11 September 1802. [GM.72.116]

HADFIELD, HOWE, in Martinique, probate, 1802, PCC. [TNA]

HAIG, WILLIAM, minister of St Andrew's, Grenada, from 1833 to 1837. [F.7.667]

THE PEOPLE OF THE WINDWARD ISLANDS, TRINIDAD AND TOBAGO, AND CURACAO, 1620-1860

HAITI, Prince JOHN of, born on St Lucia in 1786, Grand Admiral of Haiti, died there in 1817, buried in St Lucia. [GM.87.573]

HALDANE, DAVID, born 1804,son of William Haldane and his wife Jean Richardson in Galashiels, late of Turks Island, and of Buccleugh Street, Edinburgh, died in Grenada on 14 August 1838. [SG.7.702][Galashiels gravestone]

HALKET, CHARLES, born 1727, a labourer from Aberdeen, a Jacobite banished to the Leeward Islands, liberated by the French and landed on Martinique in 1747. [TNA.SP36.102][P.2.272]

HALL, ROBERT, a merchant from Glasgow, died in Trinidad on 8 January 1820. [Gad.19.2378]

HALLY, JOHN, a planter in Grenada in 1854. [NRS.SC48.49.25.54/67]

HAMILTON, ANN, spouse of Austin Leigh a minister of the Gospel in Dominica, parents of Ann, a sasine, 1772. [NRS.RS27.199.181]

HAMILTON, CHARLES, from Tobago, married Miss MacDonnell, daughter of Charles MacDonnell, in Newhall, County Clare, on 23 October 1799. [GM.69.1192]

HAMILTON, DAVID, in Grenada, probate, 1780, PCC. [TNA]

HAMILTON, ELIZABETH, born 1725, a seamstress from Banff, wife of Edward Clavering, a Jacobite banished to the Leeward Islands, liberated by the French and landed on Martinique in 1747. [TNA.SP36.102] [P.2.118]

HAMILTON, HENRY, Governor of Dominica, died in Antigua on 29 August 1796. [GM.67.164]

HAMILTON, HENRY R., Speaker of the House of Assembly in Tobago 1838. [Parliamentary Papers, 1839]

THE PEOPLE OF THE WINDWARD ISLANDS, TRINIDAD AND TOBAGO, AND CURACAO, 1620-1860

HAMILTON, ISABEL, born 1697, a knitter from Musselburgh, a Jacobite banished to the Leeward Islands, liberated by the French and landed on Martinique in 1747. [TNA.SP36.102]

HAMILTON, Reverend JAMES, a planter on Whim Estate, Tobago, in 1836. [TNA.T71.1572]

HAMILTON, JOHN, from Tobago, married Susie Wilson, daughter of William Wilson in Soonhope, in Canongate Kirk on 3 November 1775. [CMR]

HAMILTON, JOHN, of Rissland, Tobago, see deed, 1775, [NRS.RD3.244.419]; probate, 1801, PCC. [TNA]

HAMILTON, J., warden of St Andrew's parish, Dominica, in 1847. [DC27.2.1847]

HAMILTON, MARY ANNE, daughter of Dr Robert Hamilton in Grenada, married Andrew Loughnan in London on 21 June 1798. [GM.68.535]

HAMILTON, MARY, born 1742, widow of Robert Hamilton MD in Grenada, died in London on 29 October 1815. [GM.85.636]

HAMILTON, ROBERT, in Grenada, 1776. [NLS.Acc.8793/7]

HAMILTON, WILLIAM, born 1748, a merchant aboard the Campbell bound from Bristol to Grenada in December 1774. [TNA.T47.9-11]

HAMILTON, ..., daughter of Governor Hamilton, was born in Dominica in 1797. [GM.67.433]

HAMMET, FREDERIC JAMES GORDON, nephew of Sir Ralph Woodford former Governor of Trinidad, died there on 11 January 1834. [GM.104.558]

HANA, SARA, wife of Josseph Hu Hobel, died in Curacao on 10 October 1783. [Beth Hain Cemetery, Curacao]

THE PEOPLE OF THE WINDWARD ISLANDS, TRINIDAD AND TOBAGO, AND CURACAO, 1620-1860

HANDLEY, WILLIAM, in Trinidad, probate, 1812, PCC. [TNA]

HANKEY, JOHN PETER, in Grenada, probate, 1807, PCC. [TNA]

HANNAY, WILLIAM, born 1791, died in St Vincent in 1846. [Glenluce gravestone]

HARLOW, JOHN, born 1743, a gentleman and a planter from London, emigrated via London aboard the Ariadne bound for Dominica in December 1773. [TNA.47.9-11]

HARRIS, Lord GEORGE FRASER, Governor of Trinidad, married Sarah Cummins, second daughter of Archdeacon George Cummins in Trinidad on 16 April 1850. [GM.ns34.200]

HARRIS, RICHARD, in Curacao in 1720. [NRS.AC9.714]

HARRIS, ..., son of Lady Harris, was born in Trinidad in 1851. [GM.ns35.420]

HARRISON, SAMUEL, born 1786, Assistant Commissary General, died in Grenada on 8 October 1817. [GM.87.562]

HART, FRANCIS, a surgeon from Lambeth, died in Martinique on 6 March 1798. [GM.66.439]

HARTLEY, JAMES, from St Vincent, died in London on 24 October 1798. [GM.68.995]

HARVIE, FRANCIS, of Antigua, died in Dominica on 29 January 1839. [SG.8.757][SG.757]

HARVEY, JOHN, born 1753, a former President of Grenada, died at Castle Semple on 23 August 1820. [GM.90.283]

HARVEY, ROBERT, in Grenada in 1776. [NLS.Acc.8793/1]; died in Exeter on 29 July 1791. [GM.61.777]

HASFORD, ..., born in Antigua, an Assemblyman and Colonel of the Grenada Militia, died in June 1830. [St George gravestone, Grenada]

HAWKINS, GEORGE CHARLES, only son of Thomas Vincent Hawkins in Chelsea, died in Tobago on 4 December 1850. [GM.ns35.222]

HAY, JAMES, of Lower La Lante Estate, in Grenada, a deed, 8 May 1792. [NRS.RD3.256.57]

HAY, Dr JOHN, in Grenada, was admitted as a burgess of Arbroath in 1790. [ABR]; a physician in Grenada for 38 years, died in 1803. [AJ.2921]

HAY, JOHN, in Grenada, probate, 184S, PCC. [TNA]

HAY, JOHN WILSON, an Advocate from Edinburgh, Puisne Judge in Grenada, died there on 27 May 1837. [CM.18297][DPCA.1826]

HAY, Captain LEWIS JAMES, youngest son of Lewis Hay in Edinburgh, a Magistrate in Port of Spain, Trinidad, died there on 9 September 1834. [AJ.4536][GM.105.222]

HAY, LORRAINE GEDDES, born 1847, Treasurer of Tobago from 1879 to 1885, Commander of Tobago from 1889 to 1892, died in 1904.

HAY, MARGARET, in Tobago around 1847, sister of William Hay a shipmaster in Aberdeen. [NRS.PS3.16.52]

HAY, ROBERT, in Tobago around 1847, sister of William Hay a shipmaster in Aberdeen. [NRS.PS3.16.52]

HAZELL, JOHN HERCULES, born 1816, died in Mustique on 22 November 1886; his wife Ann was born in 1820, died 18 December 1889, their son Henry Arrindale Hazell, was born in 1841, died 28 November 1900. [St Vincent gravestone]

HEARTON, GEORGE, born 1747, a gentleman bound from London aboard the Crook bound for St Vincent in November 1774. [TNA.T47.9/11]

HEATH, Reverend WILLIAM, born 1782, died 26 November 1833. [St George gravestone, Grenada]

HEDDON, JAMES, Venue master of Tobago, died on 2 June 1817. [GM.87.183]

HENDERSON, EBENEZER, a merchant, planter, attorney, and a member of the Legislative Council of Tobago, from 1884 to 1888, died in 1890.

HENDERSON, JAMES, born 1717, a cook from Angus, a Jacobite banished to the Leeward Islands, liberated by the French and landed on Martinique in 1747. [TNA.SP36.102][P.2.282]

HENDERSON, JAMES, formerly in Grenada, latterly a shipwright in Greenock, later in Crawforddykes in 1810, [GA.T-ARD.13.1] testament, 1819, Comm. Glasgow. [NRS.SC53.56.2.109]

HENDERSON, JAMES B., born 1824 in Woodside, Aberdeen, a clerk in the service of McHugh and Company, died in St Lucia on 18 December 1845. [AJ.5116]

HENDERSON, JANE, widow of Thomas Henderson in Dominica, died in Woolwich on 5 April 1822. [GM.92.380]

HENDERSON, JOHN, in Dominica, probate, 1812, PCC. [TNA]

HENDERSON, JOHN, from St Vincent, married Ann Dunlop McArthur, eldest daughter of Charles McArthur, in Port Glasgow on 12 September 1831. [AJ.4367]

HENDERSON, LOGAN, a planter in Dominica, husband of Isobel Wilkie, a deed. 26 April 1773. [NRS.RD3.733.208]

HENDRIE, KINLOCH, son of Alexander Hendrie a merchant in Edinburgh, died in Dominica on 13 March 1807. [SM.69.477] [AJ.3101]

HENDRIE, THOMAS SKINNER, born 1850, son of George Hendrie a farmer [1814-1867] and his wife Jane Skinner [1826-1860], died in Trinidad on 2 April 1877. [Straiton gravestone, Ayrshire]

HENDRIE, WILLIAM, a surgeon, son of Alexander Hendrie a merchant in Edinburgh, died in Dominica in 1806. [AJ.3097]

HENDRIE, WILLIAM, a planter on Carnbee Estate, Tobago, in 1836. [TNA.T71.1572]

HENLYNE, ANDRIES, from Curacao to New York in 1699. [SPAWI.1699.680]

HENRIQUE, ABRAHAM, a merchant in Curacao, died 1726. [Curacao Beth Hain gravestone]

HENRIQUES, DANIEL COHEN, a merchant in Curacao 1750s

HENRIQUES, JEOSUAH, a merchant in Curacao trading with the New Netherlands in 1656.

HENRIQUEZ, PHELIPE, born 1660, a Jewish slave trader based on Curacao, died 1718.

HENSTON, ROBERT, returned to Grenada via Falmouth in February 1774. [TNA.T47.9-11]

HEPBURN, ROBERT, born 1784, son of Henry Hepburn, a builder in Perth, and his wife Jean Forrester, died in Tobago on 7 September 1801. [Greyfriars gravestone, Perth]

HEPBURN, WILLIAM, from St Vincent, died in Clifton on 25 January 1846. [GM.ns25.332]

HERBERT, CHARLES, born 1764, from Grenada, died 25 December 1806. [GM.76.1253]

HERTZOG, ANDREW, in Dominica, probate, 1805, PCC. [TNA]

HERVEY, JOHN, in Grenada, died 6 December 1770. [GM.40.591]

HESSEN, JAN, in Tobago or Nevis in 1678. [SPAWI.1678.849]

HESSEN, WILLEM, a lawyer who settled in Curacao in 1783. [NWIC]

HEUDE, GERARD, in St Vincent in 1773. [JCTP.1773.334]

HEUDE, MICHEL, in St Vincent in 1773. [JCTP.1773.334]

HEWITT, WILLIAM, Commissioner for the Sale of Crown Lands in Dominica, Grenada, Tobago, and St Vincent, an estate owner in Dominica, died 1781. [University of London:ms522]

HILL, JAMES, a merchant, died in Port Roseau, Dominica, in 1803. [GM.73.87]

HILL, PETER, jr, born 1791, from Edinburgh, son-in-law of Colonel Daniel McDowall, died 9 November 1829. [Kingstown Cathedral gravestone, St Vincent]

HILL, ROBERT, a merchant from Glasgow, died in Trinidad on 8 January 1820. [AJ.3767]

HINDLE, THOMAS, born 1775, died in Trinidad on 27 June 1802. [GM.72.974]

HIRRIAT, ALEXANDER, warden of St Patrick's parish, Dominica, 1847. [DC27.2.1847]

HISLOP, JOHN, in Dominica, probate, 1806, PCC. [TNA]

HOBART, GEORGE VERE, the Governor of Grenada, the second son of the Earl of Buckingham, died in Grenada on 5 November 1802. [GM..72.1225]

HOBSON, JOHN HENRY, born 1776, the Chief Justice of St Vincent, died 10 November 1829. [St Vincent gravestone]

HOCKIN, JOHN, in Dominica, third son of Reverend William Hockin in Phillack, Cornwall, married Mary Hichens, second daughter of William Hichens, in London on 24 June 1847. [GM.ns28.312]

HOGG, PETER, second son of Peter Hogg in Greenlaw, Berwickshire, died in Dominica in 1810. [EA.4864.95]

HOHEB, SAMUEL, born in Amsterdam around 1711, a merchant in St Eustatia from 1756 to 1781, relocated to Curacao by 1784. [TNA.PRO.T29/52/8]

HOLMES, JAMES, a surgeon from Paisley, died 1804 in Trinidad. [AJ.2870]

HOLMES, THOMAS, the Customs Collector in Grenada, married Caroline Benjamin, youngest daughter of Robert W. Benjamin, in Demerara on 19 November 1841. [GM.ns17.321]

HOME, FRANCIS, in Dominica in 1776. [NLS.Acc.8793.3]

HOME, JEAN, daughter of Francis Home a planter in Grenada, married James Carmichael, a merchant in Edinburgh, there on 29 May 1798. [EMR]

HOME, NINIAN, of Paxton, Berwickshire, settled in Grenada before 1766, a sasine, 1766. [NRS.RS.Berwick.15.227]; 1792. [NRS.GD267.7.1]

HOPE, JOHN, son of William Hope in Glasgow, died in Trinidad in 1817. [S.I.32]

HOPLEY, GEORGE, born in Martinique, was naturalised in South Carolina on 14 March 1831. [NARA.M1183/1]

HORNE, FRANCES KEGAN, third daughter of John Horne, married Reverend Charles Paul of White Lackington, Somerset, in Bath on 22 May 1827. [GM.96.557]

HORN, JAMES, eldest son of John Horn a gentleman in Grenada, matriculated at Glasgow University in 1793, graduated MD from Edinburgh University in 1799; a merchant in Grenada, died in New York in 1802. [MAGU.171][EMG.30][AJ.2670]

HORST, ENGELBERT, a military engineer and inspector of the fortifications of Curacao in 1767

HORT, BARBARA, wife of Major Hort of the 81st Regiment, Lieutenant General of Dominica, died in Government House, Dominica, on 16 August 1841. [GM.ns16.558]

HOSSEN, JOHN, in Tobago, 1678. [PCCol.1678.1237]

HOUSTOUN, ALEXANDER, the younger, in Grenada in 1776. [NLS.Acc.8793.41]; born 1754, a gentleman, aboard the Earl of Errol bound from Bristol to the Grenades in March 1776. [TNA.T47.9-11]; probate 1783, PCC. [TNA]; husband of Helen McKie a sasine, 1784. [NRS.RS.Wigtown.66]

HOUSTOUN, ALEXANDER, son of Alexander Houstoun a manufacturer in Glasgow, died 11 November 1821 in St Lucia. [AJ.3862]

HOUSTOUN, ANDREW, in Grenada in 1827. [NRS.GD23.6.626]; President of the Council of Grenada, died 21 December 1830. [AJ.4339][EEC.18615]

HOUSTOUN, WILLIAM, in Belmont, Grenada, Assembly Member for St Patrick's, Grenada, died in Martinique on 2 May 1842. [SG.XI.1080]

HOYES, JOHN, born 1776, late in Grenada, died in Forres, Moray, on 19 June 1839. [SG.781]

HUBBARD, Mrs SUSANNA, born 1732, widow of William Hubbard, died 19 September 1782. [Valley Chapel gravestone, Grenada]

HUMPHREYS, NATHANIEL, second son of William Hunphreys a Customs officer in Dominica, grandson of Reverend William Humphreys in Antigua, died in Dominica on 27 August 1845. [GM.ns24.551]

HUMPHREYS, W., a Customs officer, youngest son of Reverend W. Humphreys in Antigua, died in Dominica on 26 September 1835. [GM.ns4.667]

HUNTER, JOHN, born 17 April 1780, third son of John Hunter of Bonnyton and Doonholm, and his wife Jane Ferguson, settled in Trinidad in 1801, Secretary to Governor William Fullerton, died in Trinidad on 20 March 1803. [Pedigree of Hunter of Abbotshall and Narjarg, London, 1905]

HUNTER, JOHN, jr., a merchant in Trinidad, son of John Hunter the changekeeper in Marchtown, and his wife Janet Marshall, a sasine, 1818. [NRS.RS.Renfrew.14325]

HUSKISSON, GEORGE, born 1789, Customs collector of St Vincent for 30 years, brother of W. Huskisson, died in St Vincent on 7 February 1844. [GM.ns21.558][W.5.452]

HUTCHEON, ALEXANDER, born 6 November 1766, second son of Reverend John Hutcheon in Fetteresso, Kincardineshire, died in Kingston, St Vincent, on 29 October 1812. [SM.75.158][Fetteresso gravestone]

HUTCHINS, JAMES HENRY, son of Reverend James Hutchins in London, died in Martinique on 13 August 1854. [GM.ns42.638]

HUTCHISON, DAVID, married Editha Spier, daughter of Samuel Spier, of Paradise Estate, Trinidad, in Port of Spain, Trinidad, on 2 January 1834. [SG.220]

HUTCHISON, JOHN, a merchant, died in Trinidad on 18 February 1820, [GkAd.2393]

HUTTON, DAVID, a merchant in Trinidad, son of Alexander Hutton in Kinghorn, Fife, died at Savanna Grange on 25 February 1862. [FJ.15.4.1852]

HYDE, GEORGE, married Mrs Steele, daughter of Robert Burke of Prospect Lota, County Cork, in St Vincent on 7 October 1820. [GM.90.562]

IMRIE, GEORGE, born 1803, died 1828 in Tobago. [Maryhill gravestone]

IMRAY, JOHN, born 11 January 1811 in Angus, settled in Dominica 1832, died in St Aroment, Dominica on 22 August 1880. [St George church, Dominica]

INGLIS, GEORGE, a merchant in St Vincent in 1787. [NRS.NRAS.0477]

INGRAM, ARCHIBALD, Receiver General of Quit Rents in St Vincent in 1776. [TNA.T1.513.206/7; T1.521.257/8]

INGRAM, GEORGE, a smith from Banff, later in Trinidad by 1842. [NRS.S/H]

INNES, GEORGE, son of Colonel Innes, died in Grenada on 18 May 1853. [GM.ns40.209]

IRVINE, CHARLES, a sugar planter on Grange Estate, Tobago, in 1763. [NRS.CS230.misc.22.2]

IRVINE, CHARLES, from Tobago, married Rosina Edmonstone, in Edinburgh on 26 July 1794. [EMR]

IRVINE, CHARLES, a sugar planter in Tobago in 1831. [NRS.CS96.1063]

IRVINE, CLARA CHRISTIANNA, daughter of Christopher William Irvine of Bath and Tobago, died in Brompton on 31 August 1844. [GM.ns22.440]

IRVINE, ROBERT, second son of Reverend Dr Irvine in Little Dunkeld, Perthshire, died in Garth, Trinidad, in March 1830. [S.1079]

IRVINE, WALTER, in Tobago, married Catherine Gordon, second daughter of Alexander Gordon in Campbelltown, Argyll, in Deebank in 1797. [GM.67.798]

IRVING, JAMES, born 1816, son of David Irving and his wife Mary Broatch in Kirkpatrick-Fleming, Dumfries-shire, died 4 February 1841 in Trinidad. [Kirkpatrick-Fleming gravestone]

IRVING, WILLIAM, born 1790, son of James Irving and his wife Agnes Beattie in Caerlaverock, Dumfries-shire, died 2 January 1816 in Tobago. [Caerlaverock gravestone]

IRWIN, ALEXANDER BURROWES, born 1743, late of the 32nd Regiment, died 22 July 1806. [St Vincent gravestone]; in St Vincent, probate, 1807, PCC. [TNA]

IRWIN, HARRIET FRANCES, born 1785, daughter of Alexander Burrowes Irwin and wife of John Roche Dasart, died 22 January 1808. [St Vincent gravestone]

IRWIN, HENRY BURY, born 1787, son of Alexander Burrowes Irwin and his wife Lydia, a Captain of the 67th Regiment of Foot, was killed in battle in the Pyrenees on 10 November 1813. [St Vincent gravestone]

JACKSON, ADAM, born 1791, son of Andrew Jackson in Annan, Dumfries-shire, died 25 January 1808 in Trinidad. [Annan gravestone]

THE PEOPLE OF THE WINDWARD ISLANDS, TRINIDAD AND TOBAGO, AND CURACAO, 1620-1860

JACKSON, ANNA MARY, youngest daughter of Barnewell Jackson in St Vincent, and niece of Sir William Snagg the Chief Justice of Antigua, in St John's, Antigua, on 11 June 1863. [GM.ns2/15.231]

JACKSON, FRANCIS, born 1810, third son of Joseph Jackson in Orpington, Kent, the Provost Marshal of Grenada, died on 23 January 1857. [GM.ns2/2.371]

JACKSON, JOSIAS, born 1762, former Councillor of St Vincent and MP for Southampton, died in St Vincent on 30 August 1819. [GM.89.471]

JACKSON, WILLIAM, born 1725, a labourer from Angus, a Jacobite banished to the Leeward Islands, liberated by the French and landed on Martinique in 1747. [TNA.SP36.102][P.2.300]

JACKSON, WILLIAM, of St Vincent, graduated MD from Edinburgh University in 1794. [EMG.25]

JACKSON, Mr, the Attorney General of Trinidad, died there in 1844. [GM.ns23.334]

JAMIESON, JAMES, a surgeon and merchant in Tobago, partner in the firm of John Cook and Company merchants in Tobago, testament, 1783, Comm. Edinburgh. [NRS]

JAPP, JOHN, born 1731, a carpenter from Banff, a Jacobite banished to the Leeward Islands, liberated by the French and landed on Martinique in 1747. [TNA.SP36.102][P.2.302]

JARDINE, HERIOT & Co., Port of Spain, Trinidad, 1846. [TS.1.1.1846]

JA'TRUE, ..., in St Vincent in 1730. [SPAWI.1730.260iii]

JEFFERY, JOHN UNIACKE, Captain of the 81st Regiment, eldest son of T. N. Jeffery in Halifax, Nova Scotia, die in Tobago in 1841. [GM.ns16.445]

JELLICOE, JEREMIAH, Attorney General of Grenada, died there on 19 January 1817. [GM.87.374]

JEMMETT, BARRY LANCASTER, MD in Grenada, married Catherine Kingsley, daughter of Thomas Kingsley, in Langley Marsh, Buckinghamshire, on 10 December 1844. [Gm.ns23.198]

JESSOP, FREDERICK, born 1800, son of Joseph Shiercliffe Jessop, of Waltham Abbey, Essex, died in St Vincent, on 9 June 1820. [GM.90.186]

JOHNSON, JOHN, in St Vincent, died, aboard the Oaks on passage from England to St Vincent on 8 November 1820. [GM.90.570]

JOHNSON, WILLIAM N., warden of St Patrick's parish, Dominica, 1847. [DC27.2.1847]

JOHNSTON, Colonel ANDREW, Governor of Dominica in 1797. [NLS.ms5375.158-198]

JOHNSTON, ANDREW, in Dominica, a deed, 30 November 1803. [NRS.RD2.289.380]

JOHNSTONE, Lady GEORGINA COCHRANE, third daughter of the Earl of Hopetoun, and wife of Colonel Andrew Johnstone the Governor of Dominica, brother of the Earl of Dundonald, died in Rosseau, Dominica, on 19 September 1797. [EEC.418][AJ.2608][GM.67.1069][EWJ.1]

JOHNSTON, JAMES, son of William Johnston [1778-1801] and his wife Jessie Thomson [1773-1830], in Lockerbie, Dumfries-shire, died in St Lucia. [Dryfesdale gravestone]

JOHNSTONE, WILLIAM, late of Grenada, now of Paris, sold Upper Granton, St George, Grenada, to John Ross, late of Grenada, now of Aberdeen, on 24 May 1825. [Caribbeana.3.223]

JOHNSTONE, W. J., warden of St David's parish, Dominica, 1847. [DC27.2.1847]

JOINER, DAVID, a labourer from Aberdeen, a Jacobite banished to the Leeward Islands, liberated by the French and landed on Martinique in 1747. [TNA.SP36.102][P.2.306]

JOLLY, A. C., clerk of the market in Rosseau, Dominica, in 1840. [DC:1.8.1840]

JOLLY, MARTIN, born 1753, a planter, aboard the Albion bound from Plymouth to St Vincent in January 1775. [TNA.T47.9-11]

JONES, WILLIAM, born 1723, a merchant from Bristol, via Bristol aboard the Indian King bound for Tobago in December 1773. [TNA.T47.9-11]

JOURDAN, PIERRE, in Dominica in 1771. [JCTP.1773.274]

JULIE, ROSE, in Dominica in 1771. [JCTP.1773.248]

JUNOR, Dr WILLIAM, a surgeon in Grenada, married Sarah Mark, daughter of Dr Mark, in Edinburgh on 5 December 1777. [EMR]; graduated MD from King's College, Aberdeen, on 16 February 1778. [KCA]

JUSTICE, MARIA RAE CAMPBELL, wife of Alexander Stewart MD, staff surgeon, died in Dominica on 11 May 1844. [AJ.5044][W.5.497][EEC.21080]

KEARTON, ANTHONY, from America, died at Barouallie, St Vincent, on 3 July 1803.

KEATE, ..., son of Robert William Keate the Governor of Trinidad, was born in St Ann's, Trinidad, on 6 March 1862. [GM.24.579]

THE PEOPLE OF THE WINDWARD ISLANDS, TRINIDAD AND TOBAGO, AND CURACAO, 1620-1860

KEAY, WILLIAM, warden of St George's parish, Dominica, 1840. [DC27.2.1847]

KEILLER, ALEXANDER BENNET, born 1824, son of John Keiller and his wife Ann Bennet, died 27 April 1848 in Tobago. [Howff gravestone, Dundee]

KEITH, CHARLES, in Tobago, probate 1784, PCC. [TNA]

KEITH, GEORGE, a shoemaker from Aberdeen, a Jacobite banished to the Leeward Islands, liberated by the French and landed on Martinique in 1747. [TNA.SP36.102][P.2.308]

KEMLO, W., MD, born 1795, surgeon of the 79th Regiment, died in Dominica in 1840. [S.24.2124]

KENNEDY, ABRAHAM, constable in St Andrew's, Dominica, 1847. [DC:27.2.1847]

KENNEDY, CHARLES NEIL, a surgeon from Pitlochry, died in St Vincent on 4 January 1824. [FH.111][EEC.17585]

KENNEDY, DANIEL, MD, born 1815, died 2 July 1845 in Grenada. [Buchlyvie gravestone]

KENNEDY, JOHN, born 1715, a labourer from Perthshire, a Jacobite banished to the Leeward Islands, liberated by the French and landed on Martinique in 1747. [TNA.SP36.102][P.2.314]

KENNEDY, WILLIAM, born 1816, son of Thomas Kennedy, a manufacturer in Perth, and his wife Elizabeth Dow, died in June 1849 in St Vincent. [Greyfriars gravestone, Perth]

KENSINGTON, J. L., born 1789, a judge, died in Tobago on 31 August 1837. [GM.8.660]

89

THE PEOPLE OF THE WINDWARD ISLANDS, TRINIDAD AND TOBAGO, AND CURACAO, 1620-1860

KERCKRINCK, WILLEM, Governor of Curacao from 1686 to 1692, [NWIC.468.103]

KERNAHAN, A. T., a shipping agent in Port of Spain, Trinidad, 1843. [PSG.1806]

KERR, JOHN, from Grenada, died in London on 4 January 1816. [GM.86.183]

KING, ALEXANDER, son of John King, a builder, and Mary Barr in Houston, Renfrewshire, died on 23 March 1864 in St Vincent. [Houston gravestone]

KING, JOHN, from Port Glasgow, settled in St Pierre, Martinique, died on 25 December 1799, testament, 1807, Comm. Edinburgh. [NRS]

KING, JOHN, in Sherwood Park, Tobago, in 1820. [NRS.SC58.8.39]

KIRBY, FRANCIS ALVEN, son of Charles Kirby, born 1825, died in St Vincent on 1 July 1841. [St Vincent gravestone]

KIRBY, OCTAVIA, born 1820, daughter of Charles Kirkby, died in St Vincent on 16 September 1834. [St Vincent gravestone]

KIRK, ADAM, son of John Kirk in Kilmarnock, settled in St George's, Grenada, by 1811, married Sarah Crooks from Kilmarnock in 1814, died before 30 March 1817.
[NRS.GD1.632.1-14]

KIRK, JAMES, sr., a planter on Highlands and Woodlands Estates, Tobago, died 1874.

KIRK, ROBERT, from Glasgow, a merchant in Grenada, a sasine, 1853. [NRS.RS.Glasgow.3974]

KNOX, ALEXANDER, died on Westerhall Estate, Grenada, on 28 July 1843. [EEC.20654]

KOCK, WILLEM, a merchant and planter in Curacao in 1750. [NWIC.598.869]

KUKAN, ALEXANDER, born 1739, a merchant from London, emigrated via Plymouth aboard the Lovely Betsy bound for Dominica in March 1774. [TNA.T47.9-11]

LA BORDE, Archdeacon, born 1821, died 10 October 1891. [St Vincent gravestone]

LA CAQUE, PETER, warden of St Peter's parish, Dominica, 1847. [DC27.2.1847]

LA CAZE, ALIX MARIE, daughter of Louis La Caze the Attorney General of St Lucia, married Frederick George Jackson of the 21st Royal North British Fusiliers, in Castries, St Lucia, on 2 February 1864. [GM.ns2/16.520]

LA CAZE, MARIA MARGUERITE FERNANDE, daughter of Louis La Caze, married Arthur J. Hutchison, second son of William Hutchison in Cheltenham, in Castries, St Lucia, on 28 November 1865. [GM.ns.3/1.267]

LACKY, JAMES, born 1731, a weaver from Edinburgh, a Jacobite banished to the Leeward Islands, liberated by the French and landed on Martinique in 1747. [TNA.SP36.102]

LA COSTE, GEORGE, a judicial referee, died in Trinidad on 1 January 1849. [GM.ns35.335]

LA FAILLE, JEAN BAPTISTE, in Dominica in 1771. [JCTP.1773.274]

LA FOND, LEONARD, in Dominica in 1772. [JCTP.1772.319]

LE GALL, JOHN, born 1794, a Counsellor of St Vincent, died at English Harbour, Antigua, on 29 June 1851, buried in Falmouth, Antigua. [St Vincent gravestone]

LA GRANGE, C., in Dominica in 1771. [JCTP.1773.274]

LAIDLAW, DAVID, an indenture re Sugar Loaf Plantation, parish of St John, Dominica, 9 July 1823. [Caribbeana.3.309]

LAIDLAW, DOUGALD STEWART, married Henrietta D'Angleborne in Dominica on 10 December 1829. [S.14.1056]; President of the Council of Dominica in 1840. [DC:1.8.1840]

LAIDLAW, ELIZA MARY, daughter of John Laidlaw President of Dominica, married Reverend John Innes of Downe, Hythe, there on 27 April 1847. [GM.ns28.80]

LAIDLAW, JAMES, Clerk of the Council of Dominica, died there on 1 August 1841. [GM.ns16.668]; born1810, died 1 August 1841. [St George Church, Roseau]

LAIDLAW, JOHN, husband of Mary ....., an indenture re Sugar Loaf Plantation, parish of St John, Dominica, 9 July 1823. [Caribbeana.3.309]

LAIDLAW, MARY ANNE, daughter of John Laidlaw in Dominica, married Thomas Denne, in Downe, Kent, on 19 October 1852. [GM.ns39.86]

LAIDLAW, ROBERT, son of James Laidlaw of Hindleshope, died in Grenada in 1797. [GM.67.897]

LAING, JAMES, in Dominica, a sasine, 21 November 1798, [NRS.RS.Aberdeen.1858]; a planter on Macouchere sugar estate, Dominica, on 28 July 1804, [Caribbeana.3.309]; dead by September 1828, father of Susanna, Maria, Isabella and Margaret. [NRS.RD5.400.599]; born 1748, of Haddo, Aberdeenshire, late of Dominica, died in 1831. [AJ.24.4.1831]

LAING, JOHN, Captain of the St George Militia, eldest son of Thomas Laing, died in Dominica on 10 August 1808. [SM.70.1808]

[GM.78.1126]; his widow Maria, born 1778, died in Jersey on 22 February 1853. [GM.ns39.452]

LAING, JOHN, in Dominica, was granted the lands of Auchabers on 2 June 1808, [NRS.RGS.138.84.147]; Provost Marshal of Dominica, then in Surrey, England, in 1821. [NRS.CS17.1.40/256]; services of heirs, 1829. [NRS]

LAING, MARIA, born 1778, widow of John Laing of Dominica and of Haddo, Scotland, died in Jersey on 22 February 1853. [GM.ns39.452]

LAING, ROBERT, in Dominica, a deed, 4 September 1828. [NRS.RD.406.599]

LAING, THOMAS & Company in Dominica, accounts, 1805-1821. [NRS.GD126, box 1]

LAING, WILLIAM, born in Greenock, a merchant late of Tobago, died in Grenada, on 14 July 1820. [S.4.192]

LAMB, JAMES, born 1722, a watchmaker from Edinburgh, a Jacobite banished to the Leeward Islands, liberated by the French and landed on Martinique in 1747. [TNA.SP36.102][P.2.330]

LAMBERT, ..., born 1744, a servant, from London to Grenada aboard the Mary in February 1774. [TNA.T47.9-11]

LAMBERT, ..., son of Reverend George Lambert, was born in Arouca, Trinidad, on 21 June 1862. [S.2208]; Georgina, daughter of Reverend George Lambert, died in San Fernando, Trinidad, on 24 August 1863. [S.2586]

LAMONT, BOYDEN, born 1794, son of James Lamont of Knockdaw, Cowal, Argyll, died in Cedar Grove, Trinidad, on 31 August 1837. [S.1860][Cowal gravestone]

LAMONT, ISAAC, sr., a resident of Curacao in 1735. [Brieveb en Papieren van Curacao]

LAMONT, ISAAC, jr., a resident of Curacao in 1735. [Brieveb en Papieren van Curacao]

LAMONT, JOHN, in Trinidad, a deed, 6 December 1828, [NRS.RD5.376.129]; son of James Lamont of Knockdaw, Cowal, Argyll, died in Trinidad on 27 November 1850. [Cowal gravestone]

LAMONT, JOHN, of Benmore, a resident of Cedar Grove, Trinidad, a sasine in 1853. [NRS.RS.Argyll.680]

LAMONT, WILLEM, a resident of Curacao in 1735. [Brieveb en Papieren van Curacao]

LANDRETH, RICHARD, a planter in Grenada, witness to a deed in 1796. [NRS.RD3.276.249]; probate, 1810, PCC. [TNA]

LANG, HUGH, in Grenada in 1776. [NLS.Acc.8793/8]

LANG, ROBERT COOPER, born 1813, son of Robert and Maria Lang in Surrey, died 29 March 1839. [St Vincent gravestone]

LANGLANDS, DONALD, born 1776, son of George Langlands a land surveyor in Campbelltown, died in Trinidad in 1803. [CM.12866]

L'ANGLOIS, LOUIS, in Dominica, dead by 1772. [JCTP.1772.319]

LAPSLIE, JAMES, second son of Reverend James Lapslie in Campsie, Stirlingshire, was educated at Glasgow University in 1812, died on 23 August 1819 in Tobago. [MAGU.266]

LARDNER, MARIA, only daughter of J. Lardner of Barbados, married R. H. Vetch a Lieutenant of the Royal Engineers, in Dominica on 29 July 1863. [GM.ns2/15.498]

LARKINS, HENRY, born 1795, a barrister, died in Grenada on 19 December 1820. [GM.91.186]

LA ROCHE, JEAN BAPTISTE, in Dominica in 1772. [JCTP.1772.319]

LA ROCHE, WILLIAM, in Dominica in 1772. [JCTP.1772.319]LA RONDE, MORANDAIS ADENAT, constable in St Mark's, Dominica, in 1847. [DC.17.2.1847]

LASERRE, ANTOINE, in Dominica in 1772. [JCTP.79.9]

LATHAM, MARY, born 1754, a servant from London, aboard the Westerhall in Plymouth bound for the Grenades in January 1774. [TNA.T47.9-11]

LATOUCHE, CHEVALIER JOHN, constable in Rosseau, Trinidad in 1847. [DC.17.2.1847]

LA VERDAINT, NICHOLAS, and his wife Theodora, in Dominica in 1776. [JCTP.83.13]

LAURENCE, ANDREW, born 3 April 1785 in Dunottar, Kincardineshire, son of Andrew Laurence, a blacksmith in Gallowton, and his wife Catherine Beattie, died on 10 August 1802 in Trinidad. [Dunottar gravestone]

LAURENT, AUGUSTUS J., of St Lucia and St Vincent, 1870. [SVW.11.8.1870]

LAURENT, Sir FRANCIS, born 1734, emigrated from London to Grenada aboard the Mary in February 1774. [TNA.T47.9-11]

LAURIE, JOHN, born 1787, son of James Laurie in Glasgow, died in Curacao on 10 July 1809. [PC.20][SM.70.99]

LA VERDAINT, NICHOLAS, and his wife Theodora, in Dominica in 1776. [JCTP.83.13]

LAVERNAIRE, JOHN, constable in St Patrick's, Dominica, 1847. [DC:27.2.1847]

LAW, ALEXANDER, born 1782, son of James Law in Glasgow, died in Trinidad in 1802. [AJ.2854]

LAW, WILLIAM, only son of Reverend John Law and his wife Jane Murray in Innerleithen, died in Port-of-Spain, Trinidad, on 21 August 1855. [EEC.322794][Dunfermline gravestone]

LAWLER, THOMAS, and Company, merchants in Market Square, St Vincent, 1870. [SVG:11.8.1870]

LAWRIE, JAMES, born 11 December 1787, son of John Lawrie and his wife Ann McIntosh, was educated at Glasgow University in 1799, died on 10 July 1809 in Curacao. [MAGU.190]

LAWSON, CHARLOTTE, widow of Reverend George Brodie, died in the Presbyterian Manse, Port-of-Spain, Trinidad, on 14 April 1876. [EC.28591]

LAWSON, JAMES, born 1725, a workman from Lintrathen, a Jacobite banished to the Leeward Islands, liberated by the French and landed on Martinique in 1747. [TNA.SP36.102][P.2.334]

LAYBOURNE, W., Governor of Grenada, died in 1775. [GM.45.303]

LEARMONT, JOHN, with his wife Janet Jardine, and son John, emigrated from Dumfries-shire to Tobago in 1820. [CAR.2.351]

LEATHEM, ..., son of C. Leathem in Dominica, was born in London on 26 October 1858. [GM.ns2/5.627]

LE COINTRE, JEAN BAPTISTE, in Dominica in 1772. [JCTP.1773.280]

LE CURIEUX, JACQUES, in Martinique in 1688. [SPAWI.1688.1718.i]

LEDWICH, THOMAS, in Martinique, probate, 1800, PCC. [TNA]

LE DUFF, MARIET, in St Pierre, Martinique, legatee of Samuel Cunningham in 1796. [PRONI.D1108/A9]

LE FEBURE, JEAN BAPTISTE, in Dominica in 1775. [JCTP.1775.441]

THE PEOPLE OF THE WINDWARD ISLANDS, TRINIDAD AND TOBAGO, AND CURACAO, 1620-1860

LE COINTRE, JEAN BAPTISTE, in Dominica in 1772. [JCTP.79.8]

LE GRAND, Sir Samuel, Commandant of Dominica in 1736, [SPAWI.1736.361]; former Governor of Montserrat, died in 1779. [GM.49.51]

LEIGH, AMELIA, daughter of Austin Leigh a minister in Domenica, 1780. [NRS.CS16.1.179]

LEITH, ALEXANDER, born 4 June 1752, emigrated from Scotland in 1771, settled in St Vincent, Colonel of the local Militia during the Carib War, died 13 February 1798. [Kingston Cathedral gravestone, St Vincent]

LEITH, Sir JAMES, Governor of the Windward and Leeward Islands, papers, 1806 to 1820. [NRS.GD225.980-986]

LEITH, JOHN, a sugar planter in Tobago, 1831. [NRS.CS96.1063]

LEITH, RALPH JAMES FORBES, son of George Forbes a surveyor in Old Deer, Aberdeenshire, was educated at Marischal College, Aberdeen, a Member of the Royal College of Surgeons in 1863, health officer of Tobago, died in Bel Air House, Carricou, on 22 September 1868. [S.7855][MCA.II.567]

LEITH, Mrs, widow of Captain Leith of the 69th Regiment, only daughter of Governor Seton, married Captain Henry Evans, in St Vincent on 6 October 1807. [GM.77.976]

LE JEUNE, ..., to Grenada in 1768. [Cal.HOP.1768.832/945/955]

LENNIE, DUNCAN, born 1814, second son of Robert Lennie a merchant in Glasgow, a minister in Tobago from 1837 to 1844, died on 12 December 1858 in Northumberland, England. [F.7.671]

LE PLAISTRIER, C. I., Provost Marshal General of Tobago 1838. [Parliamentary Papers, 1839]

THE PEOPLE OF THE WINDWARD ISLANDS, TRINIDAD AND TOBAGO, AND CURACAO, 1620-1860

LE PLASTRIER, GEORGE, a magistrate of the Windward District, Tobago, in 1850. [TNA.CO290.4]

LESLIE, JAMES, son of James Leslie a merchant in Aberdeen, died in St Vincent on 27 September 1813. [AJ.3445]

LE SUEUR, LEONARD, in Dominica in 1771. [JCTP.1773.274]

LE VILLAUX, THEORORE, warden of St Peter's parish, Dominica, in 1847. [DC27.2.1847

] LEVY, DAVID, a planter in Curacao by 1679.

LEVY, THOMAS, partner of Richard Dobson in Liverpool, died in St Pierre, Martinique, on 6 October 1794. [GM.64.1150]

LEWIS, ROSA JANE, born 1834, youngest daughter of Lewis Lewis of Tynyllwyn, County Radnor, South Wales, died 23 March 1858. [St Vincent gravestone]

LEWIS, WILLIAM HOARE, born 1777 in Gibraltar, second son of James Lewis a Colonel of the Royal Artillery, died in Trinidad on 21 August 1803, [GM.74.478]; in Trinidad, probate, 1804, PCC. [TNA]

LIGERTWOOD, CHRISTIAN, daughter of Alexander Ligertwood in St Vincent, married James Ross from Leith, in Aberdeen on 20 October 1874. [SC.27097]

LINDSAY, JAMES, only son of James Lindsay a merchant in Tobago, matriculated at Glasgow University in 1807. [MAGU.232]

LINDSAY, WILLIAM, Governor of Tobago, died in 1796. [GM.66.618]

LINTON, Dr DAVID, formerly in St George's, Grenada, latterly in Ayr, Scotland, husband of Susanna Bell, testament, Comm. Glasgow, 11 July 1809. [NRS]

LION, JEAN JACQUES, in Dominica in 1771. [JCTP.1773.248]

LITHGOW, THOMAS, born 1741, emigrated via Plymouth to Grenada aboard the Laurent in December 1775, [TNA.T47.9-11]; a planter in Grenada in 1779. [NRS.CS16.1.175]

LITTEE, JOSEPH, in Martinique, probate, 1798, PCC. [TNA]

LIVERPOOL, FRANK, constable in St Patrick's, Dominica, 1847. [DC:27.2.1847]

LLOYD, CHARLES, Attorney General of Dominica in 1840. [DC:1.8.1840]

LLOYD, REBECCA M. E., died on Riviere Doree Estate, St Lucia, on 5 September 1850. [EEC.22057]

LOCKHART, CORA, fifth daughter of James Potter Lockhart of Dominica, married William T. Bremner a Captain of the 46th Regiment, in Dominica on 9 December 1845. [AJ.5114]

LOCKHART, EDWARD, son of the late James Potter Lockhart former President of Dominica, married Louisa Cumberland, third daughter of the late Admiral Cumberland, and grand-daughter of the late Richard Cumberland, in Dominica on 22 October 1837. [GM.ns9.222]

LOCKHART, JAMES POTTER, a Member of the Council of Dominica, married June Windle, eldest daughter of Thomas Windle of Bedford Row, London, there on 6 November 1811. [SM.73.877]

LOCKHART, J. P., a former President of Dominica, died there on 22 October 1837. [GM.ns9.222]; born 1775, died 22 October 1837. [St George church, Dominica]

LOCKHART, Mrs, wife of James Potter Lockhart in Dominica, died in Montserrat on 19 June 1807. [GM.77.888][SM.69.798]

LOCKHART, ..., daughter of James Potter Lockhart, was born in Dominica on 15 October 1813. [GM.83.498]

LOCKHART, JOHN DYER, born 1779 in Dominica, died in London on 15 September 1809. [GM.79.894]

LOCKHART, Mrs LOUISA, wife of Edward Lockhart, died in Dominic on 5 August 1843. [GM.ns.20.446]

LONDON, JOHN, in Dominica, probate, 1810, PCC. [TNA]

LONGDEN, ..., daughter of Lieutenant Governor Longden, was born in Dominica on 30 August 1866. [GM.ns.3.2.682]

LONGLEY, Major JOHN, Lieutenant Governor of Dominica, died there on 5 August 1838. [GM.ns10.566]

LOSH, EMMA LOUISE, eldest daughter of W. Losh in Trinidad, married T. Malcolm Sabine Pasley, Commander of HMS Atalanta in Port of Spain, Trinidad, on 13 February 1860. [S.1483] [GM.ns2/8.506]

LOSH, SPIERS, & Co., Richmond Street, Port of Spain, Trinidad. [TS.1.1.1846]

LOW, ALEXANDER, of Garton, died in Tobago on 29 September 1820. [S.5.203]

LOWNDES, JOHN, born 1755, the Surveyor General of Dominica, died on Mount Pleasant, Dominica, on 11 August 1819. [GM.89.472][S.148.19]

LUCAS, JOHN, from Dominica, died in Cheltenham in 1810. [GM.80.677]; in Dominica, probate, 1810, PCC. [TNA]

LULS, GERARD, the Slave Trade Commissioner in Willemstad, Curacao, in 1700. [NWIC.200.43]

LUMSDEN, ALEXANDER, MD, born 1751 in Aberdeen, died in Grenada on 12 May 1838. [SG.7.684][AJ.4723]

LUSHINGTON, G., son of W. Lushington in Chislehurst, Kent, died in Grenada on 1 February 1803. [GM.73.382]

LYNCH, SAMUEL, in Martinique, probate, 1801, PCC. [TNA]

LYON, WILLIAM, in Grenada, a sasine in 1794. [NRS.RS.Glasgow.6002]

MCADAM, WILLIAM, born 178- in Nigg, Ross-shire, son of Reverend Alexander McAdam and his wife Isabel McLeod, HM Attorney in Tobago. [F.7.66]

MCALISTER, ALEXANDER, a planter in Dominica, in 1776, [TNA.T1.520.3-4]; a deed, 4 March 1778. [NRS.RD4.278.326]; reference in Robert Graham's testament of 1780. [NRS]

MCALISTER Miss ELIZABETH, only daughter of Alexander McAlister in Dominica, married Walter Colquhoun, of Logon, formerly in Glasgow, in Dominica on 22 June 1776. [GM.46.435][SM.38.455]

MCALLISTER, WILLIAM, at Grog River, St Vincent, 1870. [TNA.CO264.9/95]

MCALLASTER, JAMES, in Dominica, probate, 1807, PCC. [TNA]

MCARTHUR, DUNCAN, in St Vincent in 1816. [NRS.SC53.56.2.130]; in 1818, [NRS.CS53.562];in St Vincent, a sasine in 1820, [NRS.Argyll.3149]; formerly a merchant in St Vincent, now in Glasgow in 1837, [NRS.SC58.59.15.1]; late of St Vincent, dead by 1842. [NRS.RS.Argyll.168]

MCARTHUR, HELEN, in St Vincent, 1838. [NRS.SC58.42.11.126]

MCARTHUR, JOHN MELVIL, in St Vincent, a sasine, 1842. [NRS.RS.Argyll.168]

THE PEOPLE OF THE WINDWARD ISLANDS, TRINIDAD AND TOBAGO, AND CURACAO, 1620-1860

MCBARNET, ALEXANDER, of Attadale and Torridon, Ross-shire, formerly a Member of the Council of St Vincent, a merchant in the West Indies, died in Inverness on 25 November 1838, [NRS.NRAS.771.B166][AJ.4744]; in St Vincent, was granted the lands of Attadale on 21 December 1840. [NRS.RGS.223.4]

MCBEATH, GEORGE, in Trinidad, co-owner of the <u>Garland of Glasgow</u> in 1801. [NRS.CE60.11.7.77]

MCCALL, JOHN, born 1771, of Cocoanut Point, second son of John McCall a merchant in Glasgow, President of the Council of St Lucia, died there on 3 February 1821. [EEC.17133][S.5.221]

MCCALLUM, WILLIAM, late a merchant in Glasgow, died in Tobago in 1804. [AJ.2973]

MCCOLL, JOHN, of Betsy's Hope, a planter, merchant, and attorney, died in Scarborough, Tobago, on 24 March 1879. [EC.29503]

MCCALL, Dr, warden of St John's parish, Dominica, 1847. [DC27.2.1847]

MCCOMBIE, ALEXANDER, born 1786, from Aberdeen, emigrated in 1806, died in St Lucia on 22 April 1865. [AJ:7.6.1865]

MCCOMBIE, ALEXANDER, the younger, eldest son of Alexander McCombie in St Lucia, married Ella, youngest daughter of Michael Cooke of Pallatine House, County Carlow, in Trinity House, Castries, St Lucia, on 20 March 1851. [AJ.5390]

MCCOMBIE, GEORGE, born 1832, son of Alexander McCombie in St Lucia, died in 11 North Broadford, Aberdeen, on 19 September 1851. [AJ.5411]

MCCOMBIE, HELEN, eldest daughter of Alexander McCombie the manager of the Colonial Bank in St Lucia, married Charles Wells, proprietor and editor of the "Palladium", in St Lucia on 21 February 1850. [AJ.5334]

MCCONNELL, GILBERT, husband of Jane [died 9 August 1783], parents of John [died 20 September 1783], Gilbert [died in August 1783], and Jane [died in August 1783]. [St John's gravestone, Grenada]

MCCONOCHIE, MARGARET, in Gatehouse of Fleet, widow of Robert Kerr in Grenada, testaments, 1814, Comm. Kirkcudbright. [NRS]

MCCORMACK, MARK, born 1731, a labourer from Moidart, a Jacobite banished to the Leeward Islands, liberated by the French and landed on Martinique in 1747. [TNA.SP36.102][P.2.28]

MCCOY, W. H., Provost Marshal of Dominica in 1840. [DC:1.8.1840]

MCCRACKEN, PETER, in St Lucia, a deed, 29 November 1828. [NRS.RD5.383.85]

MCDONALD, DANIEL, born 1728, a labourer from Inverness-shire, a Jacobite banished to the Leeward Islands, liberated by the French and landed on Martinique in 1747. [TNA.SP36.102][P.3.52]

MCDONALD, DONALD, born 1689, a servant from Edinburgh, a Jacobite banished to the Leeward Islands, liberated by the French and landed on Martinique in 1747. [TNA.SP36.102]

MCDONALD, DONALD, born 1725, a labourer from Inverness, a Jacobite banished to the Leeward Islands, liberated by the French and landed on Martinique in 1747. [TNA.SP36.102][P.3.56]

MCDONALD, Colonel DONALD, Governor of Tobago from 1803 to 1805. [NLS.ms3946.176; ms3947.13; ms3972]

MCDONALD, DUNCAN, in Wallilabo, St Vincent, 1870. [TNA.CO264.9/95]

MCDONALD, GEORGINA MARIA, daughter of John McDonald in Grenada, wife of John Royce Tomkin a barrister, died in Boulogne on 29 April 1857. [GM.ns2/2.740]

MACDONALD, Lieutenant Colonel G., Lieutenant Governor of Dominica in 1840. [DC:1.8.1840]

MCDONALD, HUGH, born 1734, from Arisaig, a Jacobite banished to the Leeward Islands, liberated by the French and landed on Martinique in 1747. [TNA.SP36.102][P.3.62]

MCDONALD, JOHN, a merchant in St Vincent in 1780. [NLS.8794]

MCDONALD, JOSEPH, born 1720, a weaver from Moray, a Jacobite banished to the Leeward Islands, liberated by the French and landed on Martinique in 1747. [TNA.SP36.102][P.3.72]

MCDONALD, MARGARET, born 1724, a spinner from Perthshire, a Jacobite banished to the Leeward Islands, liberated by the French and landed on Martinique in 1747. [TNA.SP36.102]

MCDOUAL, JOHN, was educated at the Scots College in Valladolid, Spain, 1780, a Roman Catholic priest, died in St Vincent. [RSC]

MCDOUGALL, ALEXANDER, of Westerhall Estate, Grenada, died there on 20 May 1852. [W.1344]

MCDOUGALL, ALLAN, a gardener from Strathlachlan, a Jacobite banished to the Leeward Islands, liberated by the French and landed on Martinique in 1747. [TNA.SP36.102][P.3.80]

MACDOUGALL, GORDON TURNBULL, born 1828, a planter, attorney, and a member of the House of Assembly of Trinidad from 1873 to 1877, died in 1881.

MACDOUGALL, JEMIMA, third daughter of Alexander MacDougall of Westerhall, Grenada, grand-daughter of James MacQueen in London, married Robert Baldwin, second son of Robert Baldwin in Toronto, in London on 30 August 1859. [CM.21821]

MCDOUGAL, PATRICK, from Grenada, married Janet Cooke, daughter of John Cooke a merchant in Crieff, there on 26 September 1812. [S.98]

MCDOUGALL, WILLIAM, late in Tobago, youngest son of Reverend Dr McDougall in Makerstoun, died in Antigua on 11 February 1825. [AJ.4033]

MCDOUGALL, Mrs, daughter of James McQueen in Glasgow, died in Amity Hope, Tobago, on 27 January 1837. [DPCA.1813]

MCDOWELL, ALLAN, MD, of Parkhill, St Vincent, died in Edinburgh on 16 April 1837. [AJ.4660]

MACDOWELL, DANIEL, born 1748, settled in St Vincent by 1779, Colonel of the St Vincent Militia, died 21 May 1829. [Kingstown Cathedral gravestone, St Vincent]; a merchant in St Vincent in 1799. [GA.T.ARD.13.1][S.994]

MCDOWELL, JAMES, fourth son of Alexander McDowell of Parkhill, died in St Vincent in 1803. [AJ.2921]

MCDOWELL, JAMES, second son of William McDowell of Castle Semple, was educated at Glasgow University in 1764, died in St Lucia on 30 May 1808. [Car.4.15]

MCDOWELL, JOHN, a merchant in St Vincent in 1780. [NLS.8794]

MCDOWELL, LAURENCE, in Grenada in 1800. [NRS.GD237.12.31]

MCEWAN, ANDREW, in Grenada, probate, 1806, PCC. [TNA]

THE PEOPLE OF THE WINDWARD ISLANDS, TRINIDAD AND TOBAGO, AND CURACAO, 1620-1860

MCEWAN, DANIEL KENNEDY, MD, born 1815, son of John McEwan and his wife Helen Loutit, died in Grenada on 2 July 1845. [Buchlyvie gravestone]

MCEWAN, GEORGE, a medical practitioner for 38 years in Grenada, died in 3 Frederick Street, Edinburgh, on 16 October 1834. [AJ.4529][Port of Menteith gravestone]

MCEWAN, JOHN, eldest son of William McEwan of Muckly, who died in Martinique in 1795, testament, 1813, Comm. Edinburgh. [NRS]

MCEWAN, JOHN, a planter at Mount Pleasant, Trinidad, died 23 October 1817. [AJ.3663][S.2.63]

MCEWAN, ROBERT, from Glasgow, died in Port of Spain, Trinidad, on 28 November 1843. [GSP.839]

MCFADYEAN, JAMES, a draper in Roseau, Dominica, testament, 1868. [NRS.SC70.1.139.740]

MCFAIR, JOHN, a minister sent to St Vincent in 1798. [EMA.42]

MCFARLANE, ELIZABETH, born 1717, a sewer from Perth, a Jacobite banished to the Leeward Islands, liberated by the French and landed on Martinique in 1747. [TNA.SP36.102][P.3.88]

MACFARLANE, JAMES, Mayor of Castries, a Member of HM Legislative Council, married Anna Maria Flora MacFarlane, second daughter of James MacFarlane senior, in Soufriese, St Lucia, on 14 February 1860. [S.1481]

MACFARLANE, MALCOLM [?],['Mackum Mackparly'], a witness in Curacao on 20 August 1641. [NY Hist. ms, Dutch vol. ii, 1642-1647, Reg. of Prov. Sec.]

MCFEE, HUGH, born 1717, a labourer from Inverness, a Jacobite banished to the Leeward Islands, liberated by the French and landed on Martinique in 1747. [TNA.SP36.102][P.3.172]

MCGILLIES, DANIEL, born 1735, son of Daniel McGillies in Arisaig, a Jacobite banished to the Leeward Islands, liberated by the French and landed on Martinique in 1747. [TNA.SP36.102][P.3.90]

MCGILLVRAY, CHARLES CALDER, born 26 May 1818 in Berriedale, son of Reverend Donald McGillvray and his wife Ann Allan in Kilmalie, Inverness-shire, died in Grenada on 6 April 1845. [W.6.569][Kilmallie gravestone][AJ.5082]

MCGREGOR, CHARLES, son of Grigor McGregor [1770-1854] and his wife Ann McGregor [1787-1838], settled in Trinidad. [Cromdale gravestone]

MCGREGOR, JAMES STRATHALLAN, born 1821, fourth son of Major General Sir Ewan Murray McGregor, died in Dominica on 12 January 1843. [AJ.4966]

MCGREGOR, WILLIAM GORDON, born 3 April 1801 in Grantown-on-Spey, a planter in St Vincent, died in Edinburgh on 15 September 1849. [Dean Gravestone, Edinburgh]

MCILWRAITH, ROBERT, born 1757, a merchant in Greenock, died in Tobago in January 1798. [Inverkip Street graveyard, Greenock]

MCINDOE, CHARLES, husband of Janet Buchanan, in St Vincent, then in Glasgow, a sasine, 1853. [NRS.RS.Glasgow, 3974]

MCINNES, ROBERT, born in Aberfoyle, died on Carrier Estate, Grenada, in 1817. [S.I.43]

MCINNES, WALTER, a merchant in Carriacou near Grenada in 1801, see John Barclay's will.

THE PEOPLE OF THE WINDWARD ISLANDS, TRINIDAD AND TOBAGO, AND CURACAO, 1620-1860

MCINROY, WILLIAM, born 1819, son of Peter McInroy and his wife Margaret McPherson, died in Trinidad on 9 November 1841. [Gourock gravestone]

MCINTOSH, ANN, born 1727, a spinner from Inverness, a Jacobite transported to the Leeward Islands, liberated by the French and landed on Martinique in 1747. [TNA.SP36.102][[P.3.100]

MCINTOSH, ANGUS, born 1721, a labourer from Inverness-shire, a Jacobite banished to the Leeward Islands, liberated by the French and landed on Martinique in 1747. [P.3.100][TNA.SP36.102]

MCINTOSH, DUNCAN, settled in Dominica in 1761, received a land grant in St Ann's parish in 1765, moved to St Pierre, Martinique, in July 1774; a merchant in Dominica, son of Alexander McIntosh, sasines, 1775. [NRS.NRAS.771.306; GD126. box 4; RS38.XIII.409-413]

MCINTOSH, JAMES, a minister sent to Dominica in 1771. [EMA.42]

MCINTOSH, JANE, born 1727, a spinner from Inverness, a Jacobite transported to the Leeward Islands, liberated by the French and landed on Martinique in 1747. [TNA.SP36.102][[P.3.100]

MCINTOSH, JOHN, born 1696, a fiddler from Inverness, a Jacobite transported to the Leeward Islands, liberated by the French and landed on Martinique in 1747. [TNA.SP36.102][[P.3.102]

MCINTOSH, MARY ELLIS, daughter of James MacIntosh master builder with the Trinidad Public Works Department, died in Port of Spain on 28 February 1873. [EC.27614]

MCINTOSH, PETER, born 1713, a labourer from Inverness, a Jacobite transported to the Leeward Islands, liberated by the French and landed on Martinique in 1747. [TNA.SP36.102][[P.3.100]

MCINTOSH, Miss, youngest daughter of William McIntosh in Grenada, married Chevalier le Sieur de Colleville, a French Infantry officer, in Ostend in 1791. [GM.61.1061]

MACKAY, CHARLES OLIPHANT, youngest son of Patrick Mackay a merchant in Edinburgh, died in Trinidad on 13 July 1859. [CM.21812]

MACKAY, JAMES, Paymaster of the 1st West Indian Regiment, married Catherine Jane Moore, widow of Dr John Moore, in Trinidad on 27 November 1823. [GM.9.176]

MACKAY, WILLIAM, in Tobago, an executor, 1810. [NRS.RD3.336.135]

MACKAY, Mrs, from St Vincent, married James Seton jr. in Bishop Auckland on 1 January 1799. [GM.69.77]

MCKELL, JAMES, in Grenada, married Barbara McKill, daughter of Robert McKill a canal engineer, in Edinburgh on 21 December 1781. [EMR]

MCKENZIE, ALEXANDER, born 1803, eldest son of Captain McLeod the Adjutant of the Ross-shire Militia, died on Bath Estate, Dominica, on 18 August 1825. [AJ.4063]

MACKENZIE, ANDREW, from Dominica, a merchant in Glasgow in 1792, a deed. [NRS.RD3.274.826]

MCKENZIE, COLIN, in Grenada, probate, 1801, PCC. [TNA]

MCKENZIE, DUNCAN, in St Vincent, married Elspet, only daughter of James Paul a ship-owner in Banff, there on 25 April 1837. [AJ.660]

MACKENZIE, FRANCIS PROBY STEWART, Lieutenant of the 71st Highland Light Industry and Fort Adjutant, second son of J. A. Stewart Mackenzie, died in Grenada on 21 December 1844. [W.538]

MCKENZIE, HECTOR, in Trinidad, probate, 1808, PCC. [TNA]

MCKENZIE, JANE, born 1728, a sewer from Inverness, a Jacobite transported to the Leeward Islands, liberated by the French and landed on Martinique in 1747. [TNA.SP36.102][[P.3.124]

MCKENZIE, JOHN, born 1715, a gentleman from Assynt, a Jacobite transported to the Leeward Islands, liberated by the French and landed on Martinique in 1747. [TNA.SP36.102][[P.3.124]

MACKENZIE, MARGARET, wife of Hugh Campbell a teacher, eldest daughter of Hector Mackenzie a teacher in Anderston, died on Troumassie Estate in St Lucia on 25 April 1839. [SG.8.786]

MCKENZIE, MARY, born 1727, a spinner from Lochaber, a Jacobite transported to the Leeward Islands, liberated by the French and landed on Martinique in 1747. [TNA.SP36.102][[P.3.130]

MCKENZIE, RODERICK, from Grenada, married Mary McKenzie, eldest daughter of John McKenzie of Avoch, at Avoch House, Ross-shire, on 9 October 1798. [AJ.2651]

MCKENZIE, WILLIAM, in Grenada, graduated MD from Edinburgh University in 1809. [EMG.42]

MCKENZIE, ..., warden of St Joseph's parish, Dominica, in 1847. [DC27.2.1847]

MACKIE, DANIEL, born 1729, a labourer from Moray, a Jacobite transported to the Leeward Islands, liberated by the French and landed on Martinique in 1747. [TNA.SP36.102][[P.3.108]

MACKIE, GEORGE, died in St Vincent on 1 August 1846. [AJ.5151]

MACKIE, JAMES, from St Vincent, was admitted as a burgess of Banff in 1778. [BBR]

MACKIE, WILLIAM, a merchant in Grenada in 1808. [GA.T-ARD.13.1]

THE PEOPLE OF THE WINDWARD ISLANDS, TRINIDAD AND TOBAGO, AND CURACAO, 1620-1860

MCKILLOP, JOHN, an engineer on Castara Estate, Tobago, in1863.

MCKINNON, or CAMPBELL, JOHN, born 4 December 1783, son of Reverend John McKinnon and his wife Elizabeth Campbell in Kilmoden, Argyll, settled in Tobago. [Inverkip gravestone][F.4.32]

MCKNAIGHT, THOMAS, in Grenada, a sasine, 1791. [NRS.RS.Wigtown.287]

MCKNIGHT, THOMAS, a merchant in Tobago, co-owner of the High Flyer of Greenock in 1799. [NRS.CE60.11.6.32]

MACLACHLAN, ALEXANDER, in Dominica in 1787, eldest son of William MacLachlan and his wife Anne McGhie in Kirkcudbright. [EUL. Laing Charters.3268]

MCLACHLAN, ALLAN, a planter in Tobago, witness to a deed in Shirwan, Tobago, 2 May 1792. [NRS.RD3.257.361]

MCLANE, HENRY, a minister sent to Dominica in 1764. [EMA.43]

MCLAREN, JOSEPH, a garrison surgeon, died in Dominica in February 1806. [SM.68.398]

MCLEA, DUNCAN, from Dunoon, Argyll, in Grenada, 1793. [NRS.NRAS.0876.18]

MCLEAN, ALLAN, born 1824, youngest son of John McLean a merchant in Greenock, died in Trinidad in 1838. [SG.8.741]

MCLEAN, DANIEL, a minister in St Vincent from 1862, died in Rothesay, Bute, 25 May 1876. [F.7.671]

MCLEAN, ELIZABETH, daughter of Donald McLean a Captain of the Queen's Royals, married George Beresford, ADC to Sir John Campbell, Colonial Secretary of St Vincent, there in 1848. [EEC.21689]

MCLEAN, FRANCIS J S, of the Ordnance Department, son of Lieutenant Colonel McLean in Hamilton, Lanarkshire, died in Dominica on 25 September 1802. [EA.4081.03]

MCLEAN, JAMES, born 1728, a nail-maker from Stirling, a Jacobite transported to the Leeward Islands, liberated by the French and landed on Martinique in 1747. [TNA.SP36.102][[P.3.148]

MCLEAN, JOHN, a planter in Carriacou near Grenada in 1801. [See John Barclay's will]; born 1776, a Councillor of Grenada, died in Limlain Estate, Carriacou, on 18 February 1816. [Alness gravestone] [GM.86.473]

MCLEAN, WILLIAM, born 1715, a labourer from Inverness, a Jacobite transported to the Leeward Islands, liberated by the French and landed on Martinique in 1747. [TNA.SP36.102][[P.3.152]

MCLEAY, WILLIAM, in Tobago, probate, 1802, PCC. [TNA]

MCLEISH, DUNCAN, born 1729, a pedlar from Perthshire, a Jacobite transported to the Leeward Islands, liberated by the French and landed on Martinique in 1747. [TNA.SP36.102][[P.3.152]

MCLEOD, ALEXANDER, in Dominica, 179-, testament, 1798, Comm. Edinburgh. [NRS]

MCLEOD, ALEXANDER, born 1728, a labourer from Inverness, a Jacobite transported to the Leeward Islands, liberated by the French and landed on Martinique in 1747. [TNA.SP36.102][[P.3.156]

MCLEOD, ALEXANDER, from St Vincent, married Roberta Sutherland, eldest daughter of George Sackville Sutherland of Uppat, in Tain on 26 September 1823. [DPCA.1107]

MCLEOD, ALEXANDER, born 1789, died in Waterloo House, St Vincent, in February 1861. [St Vincent Death Register.11]

MCLEOD, BARBARA, born 1831, third daughter of Alexander McLeod, died on 23 January 1853. [Trinity Church gravestone, Georgetown, St Vincent]

MCLEOD, ELIZABETH, daughter of Alexander McLeod, married George Hammond Hawtyne, in St Vincent on 23 September 1857. [EEC.21238]

MCLEOD, EVENA, fourth daughter of Alexander McLeod, married John Hill Beresford, third son of John Beresford the Colonial Secretary, in Trinity Church, George Town, St Vincent, on 26 March 1859. [CM.21719]

MCLEOD, GEORGE, son of John McLeod, late of Milne, Cruden and Company in Aberdeen, chief clerk in the government office in Castries, died in St Lucia on 14 February 1864. [AJ: 23.3.1864]

MCLEOD, JAMES, son of Hugh McLeod of Geanies, a planter in St Vincent around 1776. [NLS.19297]

MCLEOD, JOHN, born 1722, a labourer, a Jacobite transported to the Leeward Islands, liberated by the French and landed on Martinique in 1747. [TNA.SP36.102][[P.3.162]

MCLEOD, JOHN, in Tobago, appointed his wife Janet Alexander Stewart of Stewart Hall, Bute, as his attorney, subscribed in Tobago on 19 June 1815. [NRS.SC53.56.1]

MCLEOD, JOHN, born 1794, a partner in Simpson and McLeod, died in Trinidad on 22 June 1826. [AJ.4103]

MCLEOD, LOUISA, born 1838, youngest daughter of Alexander McLeod, died on 27 March 1842. [Trinity Church gravestone, Georgetown, St Vincent]

THE PEOPLE OF THE WINDWARD ISLANDS, TRINIDAD AND TOBAGO, AND CURACAO, 1620-1860

MCLEOD, ROBERT BRUCE AENEAS, son of Lieutenant Alexander McLeod in Tain, died in Turama, St Vincent, on 25 November 1831. [AJ.4387]

MCLEOD, RODERICK, born 1758 in Scotland, a clerk who emigrated via London aboard the Nautilius bound for Tobago in January 1775. [TNA.T47.9/11]

MCLEOD, WILLIAM WATSON, born 1819, nephew of Henry McLeod, Provost Marshal General and eldest son of John McLeod of Gordon's Mill, Aberdeen, died in St Lucia on 24 August 1840. [AJ.4849]

MCMAHON, Reverend FRANCIS, born 1759, Rector of St Paul's from 1784 to 1794, then Rector of St John and St Mathew in 1795, died 22 November 1827. [St George gravestone, Grenada]

MACMAHON, THOMAS, in Coull's, St Vincent, 1870. [TNA.CO264.9/95]

MCMARON, AGNES, wife of Thomas Duncan a surgeon in Grenada, died there on 23 June 1818. [AJ.3684]

MCMILLAN, JAMES, son of John McMillan [1777-1835] and his wife Ann Barker [1760-1842] in Whithorn, Galloway, died in St Vincent aged 28. [Whithorn gravestone]

MACMORAN, HUGH, in Tobago, a deed, 22 October 1778. [NRS.RD2.224/2.576]

MCMURDO, CHARLES, on HMS Amarillo, son of Captain George McMurdo of the Dumfries Militia, died in December 1808 in Dominica. [SM.71.158]

MCNEA, JOHN, in Tobago, a bond, 8 August 1769. [NRS.RD2.224/2.646]

MCNEILL, JAMES, in Tobago in 1800. [NRS.CS18.715.15]

MCNEIL, JOHN, a merchant in Tobago, partner of John Young, late in Tobago now a merchant in Glasgow, a deed, 1771. [NRS.RD2.224/2.646]

MCNICOL, DUGALD, Captain of the Royal Regiment of Foot in St Lucia, in 1832. [NRS.SC51.50.2.3.139]

MCNISH, JAMES, died in Castries, St Lucia, on 1 July 1839. [SG.8.795]

MACPETRIE, JAMES, son of James McPetrie in Aberdeen, was educated at Marischal College, Aberdeen, in 1815, a surgeon in Tobago. [MCA]

MCPHERSON, ARCHIBALD, born 1731, a cow-herd from Skye, a Jacobite transported to the Leeward Islands, liberated by the French and landed on Martinique in 1747. [TNA.SP36.102][[P.3.176]

MCPHERSON, DUNCAN, born 1711, a labourer from Inverness, a Jacobite banished to the Leeward Islands, liberated by the French and landed in Martinique in 1747. [TNA.SP36.102][P.3.176]

MCPHERSON, GILBERT, in Dominica, probate, 1803, PCC. [TNA]

MCPHERSON, JAMES, born 1725, a labourer from Aberdeen, a Jacobite banished to the Leeward Islands, liberated by the French and landed in Martinique in 1747. [TNA.SP36.102][P.3.176]

MACPHUNN, JAMES, clerk to Messrs Turner and Paul in St Vincent, died there on 4 February 1776.

MACQUEEN, DAVID, son of James MacQueen in London, died on Golden Lane Estate, Tobago, on 16 September 1848. [GM.ns30.670]

MACRAE, JOSEPH, a surgeon from Aberdeen, died in Grenada in December 1798. [EA.3688]

MACREDIE, ROBERT BRUCE, son of William MacRedie, died in Trinidad on 16 August 1848. [SG.1755]

MCSWINEY, JUSTIN, warden of Rosseau, Dominica, 1847; an auctioner in Rosseau, Dominica, in 1847. [DC27.2.1847]

MCTAVISH, JOHN G., in Tobago in 1849. [NRS.GD1.380.1.52]

MCVEAN, ARCHIBALD, born 8 March 1779 in Kenmore, Perthshire, son of Reverend Patrick McVean and his wife Elizabeth Campbell, settled in Grenada, died on 7 September 1822. [F.4.183][DPCA.1066]

MCVICAR, ARCHIBALD, born 1819, son of Neil McVicar of Ardishaig, died in Trinidad in April 1840. [Lochgilphead gravestone]

MCVICAR, Dr RONALD, late of Dominica, died in Edinburgh on 17 April 1797. [CM.11801]

MCVICAR, TORQUIL, in Tobago, probate 1788, PCC. [TNA]

MCWILLIAM, ANNA ELIZA, daughter of Alexander McWilliam late of Jamaica sometime of Grenada, died in Elgin on 26 February 1840. [AJ.4809]

MCWILLIAM, JOHN, in Grenada, a deed, 1 June 1826, [NRS.RD5.326.26]; an attorney on Grand Bacolet Estate, died in Grenada on 1 August 1826. [GM.96.477]

MACK, MANUEL, in Hillsboro, St Vincent, 1870. [TNA.CO264.9/95]

MACK, MANNY, in Craigieburn, St Vincent, 1870. [TNA.CO264.9/95]

MADURO, MOSES SALOMO LEVY, settled in Aruba in 1773.

MADURO, SAMUEL LEVY, a merchant in Curacao in 1776, husband of Sarah de Isaac Pardo y Vaz Farro. [NAN.NWIC.223/5]

MAIR, JOHN HASTINGS, born 12 October 1790, Lieutenant Governor of Grenada, died there on 21 March 1836. [GM.ns6.430]

MAITLAND, GEORGE, a merchant in St Vincent in 1799. [GA.T-ARD.13.1]

MALCOLM, ANTONY, in Grenada, probate 1766, PCC. [TNA]

MALCOLM, ..., daughter of Andrew Malcolm, was born in Grenada on 8 September 1842. [SG.11.1132]

MALLET, Mr, second son of Mr Mallet in Leicester, died in St Pierre, Martinique, in 1794. [GM.64.768]

MALLOUN, ROBERT, in Dominica, petitioned re a decision by the Vice Admiralty of Antigua concerning the schooner Young Crow Lane and its cargo of 18 slaves on 24 June 1769. [PCCol.1770.246]

MAN, Lieutenant, an engineer, from Portsmouth aboard the Grenville Bay bound for Grenada in December 1775. [TNA.T47.9/11]

MANDERSTON, NICOLAS HUNTER, youngest daughter of Mark Manderston in Dumfries, married W. Williams in St George, Grenada, on 2 May 1837. [S.1821]

MANDEVILLE, JAMES N., in Barronallie, St Vincent, 1870. [TNA.CO264.9/95]

MANEY, PETER, in Grenada in 1811. [NRS.SC48.49.3.110.114]

MANNERS, ROBERT, died in St Vincent on 16 January 1818. [S.2.64]

MANSON, WILLIAM, son of James Manson, a merchant in Rotterdam, and his wife Margaret Gray, grandson of Alexander Manson, a merchant in Thurso, Caithness, and his wife Elizabeth Munro, died 1801 in Curacao. [CFH.313]

MARLOW, JOHN RICHARD, died on Dunfermline Estate, Labay, Grenada, in November 1799. [GM.70.1004]

THE PEOPLE OF THE WINDWARD ISLANDS, TRINIDAD AND TOBAGO, AND CURACAO, 1620-1860

MARNOCH, ALEXANDER, born 1720, a shoemaker from Aberdeen, a Jacobite banished to the Leeward Islands, liberated by the French and landed in Martinique in 1747. [TNA.SP36.102][P.3.8]

MARQUES, MANUEL, in Belle Isle, St Vincent, St Vincent, in 1870. [TNA.CO264.9/95]

MARS, EDWARD, in Kearton's, St Vincent, in 1870. [TNA.CO264.9/95]

MARS, TELEMAQUE, in Lamee's, St Vincent in 1870. [TNA.CO264.9/95]

MARSHALL, ALEXANDER, a witness in Curacao on 20 August 1641. [NY Hist. ms, Dutch vol. ii, 1642-1647, Reg. of Prov. Sec.]

MARSHALL, ANDREW, a gardener, emigrated via Greenock aboard the Nancy, Captain Buchanan, to St Vincent in January 1778.

MARSHAL, JAMES, in Wallibou, St Vincent, 1870. [TNA.CO264.9/95]

MARSHALL, JAMES FORD, eldest son of James Marshall in Bath, died in Trinidad on 14 September 1800. [GM.70.1107]

MARSHAL, PIERRE, in Wallibou, St Vincent, 1870. [TNA.CO264.9/95]

MARTIN, CHARLES, in Dominica in 1772. [JCTP.1772.319]

MARTIN, JAMES, born in Aberdeenshire, 'for many years a planter in Grenada' died aboard the Ferrier bound for Tobago in 1838. [AJ.13.2.1839]

MARTIN, ORLANDO, in Coull's, St Vincent, 1870. [TNA.CO264.9/95]

MARTIN, SAMUEL, in Barrouallie, St Vincent, 1870. [TNA.CO264.9/95]

MARTIN, THOMAS, in Martinique, probate, 1801, PCC. [TNA]

THE PEOPLE OF THE WINDWARD ISLANDS, TRINIDAD AND TOBAGO, AND CURACAO, 1620-1860

MARTIN, WILLIAM ALEXANDER, born 1818, youngest son of W. A. Martin a Writer to the Signet in Edinburgh, died in Tobago on 24 January 1850. [GM.ns33.558]

MARYAT. JOSEPH, a Member of Parliament and Agent for Grenada, died in 1824. [St George gravestone, Grenada]

MASON, JOHN, a barber from Old Machar, a Jacobite banished to the Leeward Islands, liberated by the French and landed in Martinique in 1747. [TNA.SP36.102][P.3.176]

MASON, NATHANIEL, in Tobago, probate, 1802, PCC. [TNA]

MASTON, RICHARD, Governor of Tobago, died in Martinique on 26 October 1801. [GM.71.83]

MATTHEW, ANDREW, born 1715, a maltster from Perthshire, a Jacobite banished to the Leeward Islands, liberated by the French and landed in Martinique in 1747. [TNA.SP36.102][P.3.176]

MATHEW, EDWARD, in Dominica, probate, 1806, PCC. [TNA]

MATTHEW, SAMUEL, born 1837, eldest son of James Matthew of the High Court of Justice in Edinburgh, died in Port of Spain, Trinidad, on 30 November 1859. [CM.21615][EEC.23307]

MATTHEWS, WILLIAM, ["Willem Mattis"], born in Aberdeen in 1614, a soldier in the service of the Dutch West India Company, bound for Curacao, Dutch West Indies, aboard the Hope of Flushing [Vlissingen], in 1644. [GAA.NA.926.97/270]

MATTHEWS, WILLIAM, born 1769, eldest son of Mr Matthews a bookseller in London, a barrister who died in Tobago in July 1801. [GM.71.960]

MATSON, JOHN, in Dominica, probate, 1805, PCC. [TNA]

119

MATSON, JUDITH, born 1779, daughter of John Matson the Chief Justice of Dominica, died in Roseau, Dominica, on 26 September 1794. [GM.64.1150]

MATSON, Miss, daughter of John Matson the Chief Justice of Dominica, married Thomas Hutchinson, Fellow of New College, Oxford, on 18 July 1799. [GM.69.1189]

MATSON, MARY ROBERTA, born 1749, widow of John Matson the Chief Justice of Dominica, died in Sandwich, Kent, on 7 October 1812. [GM.82.405]

MAXWELL, Major BRYCE, son of Provost Edward Maxwell and his wife Charlotte Blair, died in Martinique in 1809. [St Michael's gravestone, Dumfries]

MAXWELL, JAMES, born 1774, of Orange Grove, Tobago, died in Cheltenham in 1811. [GM.81.88]

MAXWELL, JOHN, second son of William Maxwell of Carriden, died in Tobago on 22 October 1793. [NRS.NRAS.3626.530; GD171.530][GM.63.1214]

MAXWELL, PATRICK, in Grenada in 1776. [NLS.Acc.8793]; probate, 1790, PCC. [TNA]

MAXWELL, PETER, born in 1739, a planter bound from Portsmouth aboard the Unity, in July 1774 bound for Tobago. [TNA.T47.9-11];in Grenada in 1776. [NLS.Acc.8793.5]

MAXWELL, ROBERT, born 9 February 1777 in Stewarton, son of Reverend Thomas Maxwell and his wife Elizabeth Brown, died 26 November 1802 in Tobago. [F.3.126]

MAXWELL, ..., a planter in Tobago in 1800. [GA.T-ARD.13.1]

MEIKLEHAM, WILLIAM STUART, MD, died in Trinidad in 1854. [GM.ns42.201]

MELVILLE, ALEXANDER, in St Vincent, graduated MD in Aberdeen University on 26 December 1795. [AUL]

MELVILLE, GEORGINA ANNE, eldest daughter of Thomas Melville in Kingston, St Vincent, married Reverend Horatio William Laborde of Caius College, Cambridge, eldest son of William Laborde, on 2 December 1845. [GM.ns25.199]

MELVILLE, JANE, second daughter of Thomas Melville in St Vincent, married George Herbert Cox of the 53rd Regiment, in Twickenham on 17 May 1848. [GM.ns30.88]

MELVILLE, JOHN, a planter emigrated via Portsmouth aboard the Friendship bound for the Grenades in April 1774, [TNA.T47.9-11]; settled in Tobago in 1774. [NRS.NRAS.3626.16]

MELVILLE, JOHN WHYTE, in Dominica, 1807-1815. [NRS.GD126.box 8]

MELVILLE, JOHN, in St Vincent, graduated MD from Edinburgh University in 1811. [EMG.44]

MELVILLE, MARGARET ELIZABETH, eldest daughter of Dr Alexander Melville MD in St Vincent, married Joseph Billinghurst of Yapton, Sussex, on 28 March 1827. [GM.96.557]

MELVILLE, Mrs MARGARET JANE, born 1775, daughter of H. P. Cox and his wife Jane, died 10 May 1829. [St Vincent gravestone]

MELVILLE, General ROBERT, born 1723 in Strathkiness, Fife, educated at Edinburgh and Glasgow Universities, a career soldier, was granted 300 acres in Dominica in 1767. [NRS.GD126]; Captain-General and Governor of the Caribee Islands, 1763-1771, executor of Walter

Pringle's testament, 1760.; he died in England on 2 June 1766. [GM.36.294] NRS.GD126.9.2]; probate 1809 PCC. [TNA]

MENZIES, WALTER, born 1729, a flax dresser from Atholl, a Jacobite banished to the Leeward Islands, liberated by the French and landed in Martinique in 1747. [TNA.SP36.102][P.3.176]

MERCHANT, WILLIAM COPLAND, born 1821, son of Richard Merchant [1771-1822] and his wife Elizabeth Wilson [died 1854], an engineer, died in Tobago on 5 September 1862. [St Nocholas gravestone, Aberdeen]

MEYER, WILLEM, a Dutch merchant in Curacao in 1741. [NAN.OAC.172/43]

MICHEL, GEORGE, constable in Rosseau, Trinidad in 1847. [DC.17.2.1847]

MIDDLETON, ALEXANDER, born 1706, a servant from Aberdeen or Edinburgh a Jacobite banished to the Leeward Islands, liberated by the French and landed in Martinique in 1747. [TNA.SP36.102][P.3.190]

MILL, ANDREW, born 1730, a tailor from Banff, a Jacobite banished to the Leeward Islands, liberated by the French and landed in Martinique in 1747. [TNA.SP36.102][P.3.176]

MILL, Mr, a planter from the Grenades, returned here from London aboard the Friendship from Portsmouth in April 1774. [TNA.T47.9-11]

MILL, DAVID, in Tobago, a deed, 11 January 1776. [NRS.RD2.232/2.613]

MILLER, JOHANN GEORGE, from Leeuwarden, a Lutheran preacher who settled in Curacao in 1757

THE PEOPLE OF THE WINDWARD ISLANDS, TRINIDAD AND TOBAGO, AND CURACAO, 1620-1860

MILLER, THOMAS, born 1801, second son of Walter Miller in Highgate, died in Trinidad on 3 July 1840. [GM.ns14.446]

MILLER, WILLIAM, born 1801, son of Hugh Miller [1751-1824] and his wife Jean……., [1760-1830], died in Grenada on 23 March 1833. [Kilmaurs gravestone]

MILLS, HENRY JAMES, married Margaret Ann MacLean, daughter of Henry M. MacLean in Tortula, and widow of Alexander Currie, in Port of Spain, Trinidad, on 1 January 1863. [GM.ns2/14.369]

MILLS, WILLIAM, born 1725, a servant from Aberdeen, a Jacobite banished to the Leeward Islands, liberated by the French and landed in Martinique in 1747. [TNA.SP36.102][P.3.196]

MILNE, ARTHUR DUFF, born 1816 in Kincardineshire, an assistant surgeon aboard HMS Pique , died in St George's, Grenada, on 13 August 1843. [AJ.4994]

MILNE, PETER, in Tobago, probate, 1783, PCC. [TNA]

MILNE, ROBERT, from Auchlie near Aberdeen, emigrated to the Netherlands about 1696, from there with Captain Grieve to Curacao in 1698. [ACA.APB.I.568]

MILROY, JOHN, born 1784, son of John Milroy and his wife Mary McCulloch, died in Dominica on 3 June 1804. [Whithorn Old gravestone]

MILROY, WILLIAM, born 1784, son of John Milroy and his wife Mary McCulloch, died in Dominica on 3 June 1804. [Whithorn gravestone, Wigtownshire]

MITCHELL, A. P., born 1793, eldest son of Robert Mitchell the Provost Marshal of Tobago, died in Tobago in September 1812. [GM.82.670]

123

MITCHELL, ELIZABETH MARY LOUISE, born 1844, daughter of George A. Mitchell, died in Bellevue Cottage, Carriacou, on 4 November 1848. [AJ.5266]

MITCHELL, GEORGE, a minister in Grenada, 1858 to 1870. [F.7.667]

MITCHELL, GEORGE ABERCROMBY, infant son of G. A. Mitchell, died in Beasejour, Carriacou, on 23 August 1845. [AJ.5101]

MITCHELL, JAMES, born 1786, son of James Mitchell in the Bow of Battison, died in St Vincent on 29 December 1821. [AJ.3872]

MITCHELL, ROBERT, a planter in Tobago in 1800. [GA.T-ARD.13.1]

MITCHELL, SAMUEL, President of Grenada, marred Mary Floud, sister of Thomas Floud the Mayor of Exeter, on 7 September 1802. [GM.72.877]; Samuel died in Newport, Exeter, on 4 February 1805. [GM.75.189]

MITCHELL, THOMAS, born 1750, a blacksmith from Edinburgh, from London aboard the Greyhound bound for Dominica in December 1773. [TNA.T47]

MITCHELL, WILLIAM, born 1766, son of William Mitchell and his wife Jean Deas in Maryton, Kincardineshire, died in Grenada on 19 February 1823. [Maryton gravestone]

MITCHELL, WILLIAM JAMES, infant son of George A. Mitchell, died in Bellevue Cottage, Carriacou, on 9 December 1847. [AJ.5222]

MITCHELL, ..., daughter of G. A. Mitchell, was born in Carriacou on 2 May 1851. [AJ.5397]

MITCHELL, ..., daughter of Reverend George Mitchell, was born in St George, Grenada, on 4 June 1868. [S.7776]

MOE, Reverend SAMUEL ROUS, of St John's in Grenada, died in London on 27 May 1842. [GM.ns18.215]

MOFFAT, ..., daughter of John S. Moffat, was born in Soufriere, St Lucia, on 8 May 1849. [SG.18.1828]

MOIR, WILLIAM, born 5 October 1777, son of George Moir in Cruden, Peterhead, was educated at King's College, Aberdeen, in1792, a writer in Edinburgh and in Trinidad. [KCA.2.374]

MONDESIR, THURET, in St Vincent in 1764. [JCTP.1764.283]

MONLOUIS, LOUIS MARTIN, in Grenada in 1769. [JCTP.1769.156]

MONRO, DUNCAN, born 1728, a labourer from Inverness, a Jacobite banished to the Leeward Islands, liberated by the French and landed on Martinique in 1747. [TNA.SP36.102][P.3.204]

MONTEITH, ARCHIBALD DOUGLAS, son of Walter Monteath of Kipp, Stirlingshire, emigrated to St Vincent in 1775. [NRS.RD4.218.870]

MONTEATH, WILLIAM, born 5 November 1769,fourth son of Reverend John Monteath and his wife Anne Fullarton in Houston, Renfrewshire, educated at Glasgow University around 1785, a surgeon, died in St Vincent on 16 August 1793. [Caribbeana.4.17] [F.3.140]

MONTGOMERIE, JOHN, son of John Montgomerie and his wife Marion Paterson in Ardrossan, settled in Trinidad, married Bethia Edmonstone, parents of Hugh Montgomerie, died 1830 in New York. [HAF.1.231]

MONTRICHARD, GABRIEL, an executor in Trinidad, 1846. [NS.1.1.1846]

MOORE, CATHERINE JANE, widow of Dr John Moore, married James Mackay, Paymaster of the 1st West Indian Regiment, in Trinidad on 27 November 1823. [GM.94.176]

THE PEOPLE OF THE WINDWARD ISLANDS, TRINIDAD AND TOBAGO, AND CURACAO, 1620-1860

MORRIS, DAVID, born 1793, son of William Morris and his wife Elizabeth Simpson, died 18 May 1819 in Dominica. [Kemback gravestone, Fife]

MOQUET, FRANCOIS, in Grenada in 1769. [JCTP.1769.156]

MORALES, ISHAC DAVID, died in Curacao on 15 June 1782. [Beth Hain Cemetery, Curacao]

MORANDAIS, LOUIS LAMBERT, in Dominica in 1772. [JCTP.79.8/280]

MOREAU, EUSEBE, constable in St Patrick's, Dominica, 1847. [DC:27.2.1847]

MORGAN, CHARLES, born 1729, a barber from Elgin, a Jacobite banished to the Leeward Islands, liberated by the French and landed on Martinique in 1747. [TNA.SP36.102][P.3.208]

MORGAN, JONATHAN, born 1762, from St Vincent, died in Bath on 24 July 1843. [GM.ns20.331]

MORRIN, JANET, born 1818, daughter of John L. Morrin and his wife May, died 12 September 1836. [St Vincent gravestone]

MORON, ARON HENRIQUES, a merchant, ship-owner and ship insurance agent, settled in Curacao 1730. [NAN.OAC.192/149]

MORRIS, HENRY, a vintner in Tobago in 1800. [GA.T-ARD.13.1]

MORRIS, WILLIAM, a planter in Tobago in 1800. [GA.T-ARD.13.1]

MORRISON, ALEXANDER, born in 1826 in Turriff, died in Kingston, St Vincent, on 1 November 1863. [AJ.9.12.1863]

MORRISON, GEORGE, in Tobago, a sasine, 26 July 1800. [NRS.RS.Aberdeen.2157]; late in Tobago, 1814, son of Alexander

Morrison of Bogrie who died in September 1801. [NRS.NRAS.3585.4.2.32]

MORRISON, JAMES, a merchant in Tobago, a sasine, 3 January 1800, [NRS.RS.Aberdeen.2157]; in 1801. [NRS.RS8.GR628.52; NRAS.3585.7.11.2]

MORRISON, JAMES, MD, born in Inverurie, late of the East India Company, later a farmer in the Vale of Alford, emigrated to Grenada in 1858, died at the Carenage, Grenada. On 2 January 1860. [AJ.8.2.1860]

MORRISON, JESSIE, second daughter of William Morrison, Queen's Terrace, Ayr, married James Drennan from Springfield, in San Fernando, Trinidad, on 5 June 1878. [EC.29254]

MORISON, WILLIAM, a saddler from Glasgow, died in Grenada on 18 June 1831. [GkAd.3683]

MOSSOP, SAMUEL, born 1794, third son of Reverend John Mossop in Deeping St James, Lincolnshire, died in St Lucia in October 1809. [GM.79.1235]

MOTTA, JUDAH ANAS, born 1779 in Curacao, a merchant in Charleston, South Carolina, was naturalised in South Carolina on 7 January 1817. [NARA.M1183/1]

MOURILLON, STEPHEN, constable in St Andrew's, Dominica, 1847. [DC:27.2.1847]

MOWAT, CHARLES EGGLESTONE, second son of James Mowat a merchant in Aberdeen, died in Tobago on 27 February 1836. [AJ.4607]

MOWAT, JOHN, from Edinburgh, later in St Vincent, died in Edinburgh on 16 November 1843. [EEC.20690]

THE PEOPLE OF THE WINDWARD ISLANDS, TRINIDAD AND TOBAGO, AND CURACAO, 1620-1860

MUIR, DAVID, in St Vincent, probate, 1794, PCC. [TNA]

MUIR, FREELAND, son of Andrew Muir, a merchant in Kirkcudbright, and his wife Ann Blair, died in St Vincent in June 1797. [AJ.2609]

MUIR, JAMES, a minister in Grenada from 1884 to 1887. [F.7.667]

MUIR, JAMES BOND, only son of William Muir a merchant in Grenada, died in Chester in 1809. [SM.71.319]

MULATTRE, ETIENNE POINT, constable in St Patrick's, Dominica, 1847. [DC:27.2.1847]

MULLATTRE, VICTOR POINT, constable in St Patrick's, Dominica, 1847. [DC:27.2.1847]

MUNDAY, MARIAN CATHERINE, eldest daughter of Major Robert Miller Munday the Lieutenant Governor of Grenada, married Major Charles Knight, from Somerset, in Grenada on 10 April 1866. [GM.ns3/1.900]

MUNRO, COLIN, born 1758, late in Grenada, died 18 October 1823. [Greyfriars gravestone, Inverness][DPCA.1108]

MUNRO, DOROTHEA, only daughter of Hugh Munro in Carricou near Grenada, married John Spain a merchant in Bristol, in Clifton on 2 November 1796. [GM.66.965]

MUNRO, ELIZA, daughter of Matthew Munro in Grenada, married Captain Robert Aitchison of the Royal Navy, in Eling, Hampshire, on 18 December 1821. [S.258.415]

MUNRO, FRANCES, widow of Alexander Trinidad, eldest daughter of J. Townsend-Pasea, married Lieutenant Colonel Simms late of the 41st Regimen, in London on 8 July 1847. [GM.ns.28.312]

MUNRO, GEORGE GUNN, born 1779, a Member of the Council of Grenada, died 5 November 1829. [St George gravestone, Grenada]

MUNRO, GILBERT, born 1778, from St Vincent, died in Weymouth, Dorset, on 21 June 1843. [GM.ns20.218]; on 13 October 1823, in St Vincent, he renounced being an executor to the will of Robert Paul.

MUNRO, HUGH, from Grenada, married Isabella Dallas, daughter of Peter Dallas, in Canongate Kirk, Edinburgh, on 13 January 1770. [CMR]

MUNRO, JAMES, Captain of the Tiger of Leith died in Dominica on 9 June 1844. [W.5482]

MUNRO, JOHN, formerly in Grenada and in Trinidad, died in Buccleuch Place, Edinburgh, on 22 June 1831. [EEC.18666]

MUNRO, Captain MATTHEW, born 1761, settled in Carriacou, died on 1 February 1797, probate 1797, PCC. [TNA]

MUNRO, RACHEL SOPHIA, widow of Gilbert Munro in St Vincent, married Colonel Sir Richard Doherty, in London on 8 July 1845. [GM.ns24.416]

MURDOCH, GEORGE, second son of George Murdoch in Glasgow, died in Grenada on 10 December 1771. [SM.34.109]

MURRAY, BRUTUS, born 1797, a planter and Justice of the Peace in Tobago, died in 1887.

MURRAY, EDWARD, second son of Henry Murray in London, and grandson of Henry Murray in Trinidad, married Grace, only child of Sir Thomas Elmsley Croft, grand-niece of Lord Denman, in London on 5 March 1846. [GM.ns25.535]

MURRAY, HENRY, youngest son of Alexander Murray of Ingleston, died in Trinidad in 1817. [S.I.34]

THE PEOPLE OF THE WINDWARD ISLANDS, TRINIDAD AND TOBAGO, AND CURACAO, 1620-1860

MURRAY, JAMES W. MCD., a Customs officer in Tobago, former Assemblyman and proprietor of Calder Hall Estate, only brother of Mr Murray the harbour engineer at Sunderland, died on 26 January 1841. [GM.ns15.558]

MURRAY, JEAN, daughter of William Murray, a merchant in Edinburgh, and his wife Janet Shaw, and wife of Daniel Stewart a surgeon in Dominica, a deed, 1778. [NRS.RD4.223/1.624]

MURRAY, JOHN, born 1717, a weaver from Annandale, a Jacobite banished to the Leeward Islands, liberated by the French and landed on Martinique in 1747. [TNA.SP36.102]

MURRAY, JOHN, formerly a porter merchant in Edinburgh, died in Grenada in November 1815. [EEC.17275]

MURRAY, RICHARD HENRY, a barrister, eldest son of Thomas Murray, MD, in Trinidad, married Georgina Woodall, youngest daughter of Robert Woodall in Ardwick, Lancashire, in London on 2 February 1859. [GM.ns2/6.315]

MURRAY, Mrs, born 1784, widow of H. Murray in Woodbrook, Trinidad, died in Port of Spain, Trinidad, on 5 February 1868. [GM.ns3/5.684]

MUTER, JAMES, born 7 March 1774, son of Reverend Robert Muter and his wife Agnes Freeland, a merchant in St Lucia. [F.2.418]

MUTER, PETER, born 12 June 1783, son of Reverend Robert Muter and his wife Agnes Freeland, a merchant in St Lucia. [F.2.418]

MUTER, WILLIAM, born 8 May 1793, son of Reverend Robert Muter and his wife Agnes Freeland, a merchant in St Lucia. [F.2.418]

NAILER, CHARLES, Customs Controller, died in Dominica on 25 April 1812. [GM.82.668]

NANTON, Mrs ROSALIE, wife of John George Nanton, died on 20 September 1845. [St Vincent gravestone]

NAPIER, CHRISTOPHER, a physician and surgeon in Grenada, son of Christopher Napier, an Excise officer in Prestonpans, a deed, 1790. [NRS.RD2.250.599]

NAPIER, JOSEPH, born 1759 in the Grenades, from London aboard the Marquis of Rockingham bound from London to the Grenades in November 1774. [TNA.T47.9/11]

NAPIER, MARGARET, eldest daughter of Dr Robert Napier in Grenada and of Bervie in Scotland, died in Montrose on 24 April 1863. [S.2450]

NAPIER, THOMAS, son of Archibald Napier in Tobago, was educated at King's College, Aberdeen, graduated MA in Aberdeen on 29 March 1811. [AUL][KCA.2.402]

NAUGHTON, ALEXANDER, died in Tobago in 1829. [NRS.S/H.1865]

NEATE, RICHARD, Trinidad, probate, PCC, 1801. [TNA]

NEIL, ANDREW, Captain of the 99th Regiment, married Louisa Patey, youngest daughter of James Patey of Reading, in St Vincent in 1813. [GM.83.87]

NEIL,...., born 1756, a merchant from London, emigrated aboard the Proudfoot bound via Plymouth for Grenada in October 1774. [TNA.T47.9/11]

NEILSON, JAMES, born 1721, a labourer from Aberdeen, a Jacobite banished to the Leeward Islands, liberated by the French and landed on Martinique in 1747. [TNA.SP36.102]

THE PEOPLE OF THE WINDWARD ISLANDS, TRINIDAD AND TOBAGO,
AND CURACAO, 1620-1860

NEILSON, JOHN, from Glasgow, second son of James B. Neilson in
Queenshill, Kirkcudbright, died in Trinidad on 16 August 1853.
[EEC.22488][S.24.9.1853]

NESBIT, ALEXANDER, from Tobago, graduated MD from Marischal
College, Aberdeen, on 7 January 1820. [MCA]

NESS, ESTHER, wife of Henry Stewart, died in Williamvale, Trinidad,
on 21 December 1844. [W.545]

NEWCOMBE, FREDERICK, son of Dr Newcombe the Dean of
Rochester, husband of Elizabeth Neate third daughter of Reverend
Richard Neate in Whestone, Middlesex, the Secretary of Grenada,
died there on 25 November 1795. [GM.68.626]

NEWTON, THOMAS HENRY, born 1823, only son of T. G. Newton in
Hereford, a Customs officer and private secretary to the Lieutenant
Governor of Tobago, died there on 4 July 1843. [GM.ns20.446]

NIBBS, OCTAVIUS, a Councillor of Tobago, died on Tortula on 25
March 1789. [GM.59.573]

NICOL, ARCHIBALD, a planter in Tobago in 1800. [GA.T-AD.13.1]

NICOL, FRANCIS, son of Kenneth Nicol in Tobago, was educated at
King's College, Aberdeen, from 1800 to 1804. [KCA.2.387]

NICHOLAS, PIERRE, constable in St Patrick's, Dominica, 1847.
[DC.27.2.1847]

NICHOLLS, EDWARD, of St Vincent, married Silias Jane Wilson,
daughter of Alexander Wilson of Redhill, Middlesex, in Barnwell on
20 May 1847. [GM.ns28.200]

132

NICHOLL, GEORGE, born 1721, a weaver from Aberdeen, a Jacobite banished to the Leeward Islands, liberated by the French and landed on Martinique in 1747. [TNA.SP36.102][P.3.226]

NICHOLSON, GEORGE, born 1747, a merchant in London, from London aboard the Simond bound for the Grenades in November 1774. [TNA.T47.9/11]

NICHOLSON, JAMES, Clerk of the Assembly of Tobago in 1838. [Parliamentary Papers, 1839]

NICOLLS, O., in Grenada, a letter, 4 December 1785. [NRS.GD216.232]

NOLAN, ARCHIBALD BUCHANAN, died in Tobago on 30 August 1839. [EEC.19963]

NOLONIER, ..., born 1735, an ecclesiastic, from London, aboard the Reward bound from Plymouth to Grenada in January 1775. [TNA.T47.9/11

NORTON, ROBERT, born 1751, a labourer from Shropshire, emigrated via London on the Trecothick bound for the Grenades in January 1774. [TNA.T47.9-11]

NORTON, WILLIAM, born 1695, formerly a planter in Dominica, died in Exeter in 1782. [GM.52.551]

NUGENT, OLIVER, in Dominica in 1772. [JCTP.79.8/9]

OCHTERLONY, ALEXANDER, in Dominica in 1771. [JCTP.78.183]

O'CONNOR, CHARLES, born 1746, a planter from London, aboard the Le Soy Planter bound from Plymouth to Dominica in January 1774. [TNA.T47.9-11]

O'DONNELL, WILLIAM L., a barrister, eldest son of Nicholas O'Donnell in Dublin, died in Grenada on 2 November 1866. [GM.ns3/3.115]

O'DRISCOLL, DORINDA, eldest daughter of John O'Driscoll the Chief Justice of Dominica, married Edwin Wing of Bourton on the Water, Gloucestershire, in Taunton on 24 November 1842. [GM.ns19.197]

O'DRISCOLL, JOHN, Chief Justice of Dominica, died there on 3 June 1828. [GM.98.94]

OGILVIE, FELICITY, born 1782 in Carriacou, died in Auchenfree, Dunbartonshire, on 26 May 1831. [Cardross gravestone]

OLIPHANT, GEORGE, born on 6 June 1755 in Bower, Caithness, son of Reverend Alexander Oliphant and his wife Margaret Brodie, died in Grenada in June 1773. [F.7.115]

ORD, Sir JOHN, former Governor of Dominica, married Miss Frere, daughter of John Frere, in London on 2 December 1793. [GM.63.1148]

ORD, PETER, in Grenada, probate, 1785, PCC. [TNA]

ORDE, THOMAS, Customs Collector, Colonel of Militia, and Receiver General in St Lucia, died in St Pierre, Martinique, in 1799, [GM.69.819]; probate, 1803, PCC. [TNA]

ORR, DUNCAN, born 1706, a labourer from Perthshire, a Jacobite banished to the Leeward Islands, liberated by the French and landed on Martinique in 1747. [TNA.SP36.102][P.3.244]

ORR, DUNCAN, born 1733, a labourer from Perthshire, a Jacobite banished to the Leeward Islands, liberated by the French and landed on Martinique in 1747. [TNA.SP36.102][P.3.244]

ORR, JAMES, a planter in Tobago, a witness in 1777. [NRS.RD4.775/1.589]

ORR, MATTHEW, died on King's Bay Estate, Tobago, on 1 August 1790. [GM.60.956]

ORR, ROBERT, in Grenada, probate, 1781, PCC. [TNA]

OSWALD, CATHERINE WHYTE, daughter of James Oswald superintendent of the Inland Revenue in Elgin, married John Collie a planter in Couva, in Port of Spain, Trinidad, on 10 December 1860. [S.1743]; she died on Perseverance Estate, Couva, Trinidad, on 18 September 1863. [S.2600]

OTTLEY, ALICE, sister of Dreury Ottley, the President of St Vincent, died in Bath on 27 August 1843. [GM.ns20.444]

OTTLEY, FREDERICK, second son of Warner Ottley of London and St Vincent, died there on 27 August 1842. [GM.ns19.110]

OTTLEY, SARAH ELIZABETH, widow of Richard Ottley in St Vincent, died in London on 14 March 1825. [GM.95.379]

OTTLEY, W., born 1797, son of Dreury Ottley the President of St Vincent, and brother of Sir Richard Ottley, died in St Vincent on 24 April 1820. [GM.90.638]

PAGAN, WILLIAM, from Dominica, married Catherine Hart, daughter of the late Reverend John Hart, in Kirkenner on 23 June 1791. [GM.61.871] [NB according to the Canongait Marriage Register the marriage took place there on 16 August 1791.]

PALAIRET, ELIAS JOHN, in Grenada before 1774. [JCTP.1774.390]

PALMER, APHRA MARIA, daughter of John Palmer the Colonial Treasurer, died in Dominica on 17 May 1853. [GM.ns.40.209]

PALMER, MARY ANNE, sister of John Palmer the Colonial Treasurer, died in Dominica on 4 May 1853. [GM.ns.40.209]

PALMER, MARY, daughter of John Palmer the Colonial Secretary, died in Dominica on 17 May 1853. [GM.ns40.209]

PANTIER, PIERRE, in Dominica in 1773. [JCTP.1773.334]

PARDO, JOSIAU DE DAVID, a rabbi who settled on Curacao in 1674.

PARISE, THERESE, in Dominica in 1772. [JCTP.1772.319]

PARK, JOHN, a merchant in Dominica, a deed, 1 January 1785. [NRS.RD2.241.1.103]

PASLEY, SNODGRASS, & Co., Port of Spain, Trinidad, 1846. [TS:1.1.1846]

PATERSON, CHARLES, son of George Paterson MD, in Grenada, was educated at King's College, Aberdeen, from 1821 to 1824. [KCA.2.443]

PATERSON, EDWARD, son of George Paterson MD, in Grenada, was educated at King's College, Aberdeen, in 1823. [KCA.2.450]

PATERSON, FERGUS, in Grenada in 1776. [NLS.Acc.8793.30];in Grenada, probate, 1788, PCC. [TNA]

PATERSON, GEORGE, a physician in Grenada, witness to a deed in 1796. [NRS.RD3.276.249]

PATERSON, GEORGE, son of George Paterson MD, in Grenada, was educated at King's College, Aberdeen, from 1815 to 1816. [KCA.2.423]

PATERSON, JAMES, son of George Paterson MD, in Grenada, was educated at King's College, Aberdeen, from 1820 to 1824. [KCA.2.441]

PATERSON, ROBERT, a hosier from Old Machar, a Jacobite banished to the Leeward Islands, liberated by the French and landed on Martinique in 1747. [TNA.SP36.102][P.3.248]

PATERSON, ROBERT, born 1779, son of Robert Paterson and his wife Rosetta Maitland, died on Great Courland Estate, Tobago, on 23 July 1803. [St Andrews Cathedral gravestone, Fife]

PATERSON, WILLIAM, died in Trinidad in 1804. [AJ.2945]

PATEY, LOUISA, youngest daughter of Sir James Patey in Reading, married Andrew Neil, a Captain of the 99th Regiment, in St Vincent in 1813. [GM.83.87]

PAUL, ANNE, eldest daughter of Robert Paul the President of St Vincent, married Major Wilby of the 90th Regiment, in St Vincent on 3 February 1814. [GM.84.406]

PAUL, ELIZABETH, daughter of the Governor of St Vincent, married Captain Bent of the 5th Regiment in 1822. [GM.93.79]

PAULL, JOHN ALEXANDER, born 1842, son of George Paull of Newseat, Aberdeenshire, died on Calder estate, St Vincent, on 30 April 1803. [St Nicholas gravestone, Aberdeen]

PAUL, ROBERT, born 1746, President of the Council of St Vincent, died on 13 September 1823. [St Vincent gravestone]; a sugar planter on Kingstown Estate, St Vincent, will dated 28 August 1823, refers to his wife Elizabeth Warner, executors Gilbert Munro, Alexander Cumming, Alexander Innis; his children Charles, Elizabeth, Ann. [St Vincent]

PAXTON, ..., born 1804, Lieutenant Colonel of the 69th Regiment, died in Trinidad on 24 August 1853. [EEC.22489]

PAYARD, ELINOR, in Dominica in 1771. JCTP.1773.248]

PAYARD, PIERRE, in Dominica in 1771. [JCTP.1773.248]

THE PEOPLE OF THE WINDWARD ISLANDS, TRINIDAD AND TOBAGO, AND CURACAO, 1620-1860

PEARSON, THOMAS, born 1748, a planter from London, bound aboard the Charming Nancy from Plymouth bound for Tobago in May 1775. [TNA.T47.9/11]

PEARSON, Mr, from Manchester, died in St Pierre, Martinique, on 5 October 1794. [GM.64.1150]

PECHEREA, ..., in St Vincent in 1730. [SPAWI.260iii]

PELLETIER, JOHN, in Dominica in 1776. [JCTP.83.13]

PENRICE, HENRY, born 1819, fourth son of Dr George Penrice in Great Yarmouth, died in St Lucia on 21 September 1842. [GM.ns19.556]

PERKINS, JOHN, a merchant from Leith, a Stipendiary Magistrate in Tobago, died there on 5 June 1837. [DPCA.1823]

PERRY, Commander of the US Navy, died in Trinidad on 23 August 1819. [GM.89.378]

PERRY, WILLIAM, son of William Perry a notary in Trinidad, was educated at King's College, Aberdeen, in 1823. [KCA.2.451]

PESCHIER, JOHN, born 1744, a planter from London, with his wife born 1750, aboard the Reward bound from Plymouth to Grenada in January 1775. [TNA.T47.9/11

PESCHEUR, JULLIEN, in Martinique in 1688. [SPAI.1688.1718.iii]

PETIT, JEAN BAPTISTE, in Dominica in 1772. [JCTP.79]

PETRIE, JAMES, born 1727, a labourer from Angus, a Jacobite prisoner banished to the Leeward Islands, liberated by a French privateer and landed in Martinique in 1747. [TNA.SP36.102]

PETRIE, JOHN, born 1745, a planter, from Plymouth aboard the London bound for Tobago in January 1775. [TNA.T47.9-11]

PETTY, JOHN, born 1749, a distiller from London, emigrated via London aboard the Friendship bound for the Grenades in April 1774. [TNA.T47.9-11]

PHILIP, JOHN BAPTIST, MD, died in Trinidad on 16 June 1829. [GM.99.190]

PHILIP, MARY, born 1808, wife of St Louis Philip, died in Bushy Park, Nasgarina, Trinidad, in 1843. [GM.ns19.556]

PHILIPS, JAMES W., in Port of Spain, Trinidad, 1846. [TS:1.1.1846]

PHIMISTER, JOHN, son of Robert Phimister in Bishopmill, Elgin, died in Mount Pleasant Estate, St Vincent, on 27 September 1847. [AJ.5212]

PICTON, Sir THOMAS, Governor of Trinidad, a letter, 1799. [NLW.ms.1410]

PIERRE, JOHN, a slave of William Phillip in Grenada, letters of manumission, 1811. [EUL.Laing.II.79/5]

PIETERS, SIJTGE, from Amsterdam aboard the Jacob bound for Brazil, married Cornelis de Boer, gunner of the Barquelange at St Vincent, sailed to Curacao, returned to Amsterdam before 1645. [SAA.NA.1291/193]

PIGOTT, JAMES, Attorney General of Tobago, and Admiralty Judge of England, died in Tobago on 17 January 1807. [GM.77.376]

PINEDO, GABRIEL, a planter at Wacau, Curacao, in 1792. [NWIC566.556]

PINEDO, MANUEL HISQUIANA, a ship-owner in Curacao in 1767. [NAN.OAC.1560/215]

PINTARD, PONTIUS STILL, gentleman in St George, Grenada, will 24 October 1774, estate left to Anthony Van Dam and Lewis Pintard merchants in New York as trustees. [Caribeanna.3.222]

PINTO, JEISUAH, a cantor from Amsterdam, settled in Curacao in 1815.

PIRRY, JAMES, a merchant in Trinidad, co-owner of the Maria of Greenock, in 1800. [NRS.CE60.11.6.9]

PITMAN, WILLIAM, constable in Rosseau, Trinidad in 1847. [DC.17.2.1847]

PLUMMERIDGE, CHARLES WILLIAM, born 1830, died 26 October 1850. [St Vincent gravestone]

PLUMMERIDGE, JOHN JASPER, born 4 July 1828, husband of Leonora Margaret Plummeridge, a merchant and an Assemblyman, died 5 April 1883. [St Vincent gravestone]

POLLOCK, WILLIAM, a mason and wright in Tobago, dead by 1775, son of William Pollock, a farmer in Shielhill, and his wife Mary Spreull, see deed. [NRS.RD3.244.419]

POLSON, DAVID, Secretary to the Governor of Dominica, died in 1777. [GM.48.607][SM.40.628]

PORTER, ROBERT, died on the Adelphi Estate, St Vincent, on 14 January 1820. [GM.90.281]

PORTER, WILLIAM, born 1815, son of Francis Porter a farmer in Auchintender, Forgue, was educated at King's College, Aberdeen, graduated MA in March 1835, a merchant in St Vincent, died 22 February 1847, at Mount Pleasant, St Vincent. [KCA.290] [AJ.5178]

THE PEOPLE OF THE WINDWARD ISLANDS, TRINIDAD AND TOBAGO, AND CURACAO, 1620-1860

POSTLETHWAITE, WILLIAM, in Dominica, probate, 1805, PCC. [TNA]

POWELL, T., born 1791, the Assistant Commissary General, died in Grenada on 17 September 1817. [GM.87.561]

PREVOST, GEORGE, Governor of Dominica, a latter to Horatio Nelson, 1805. [BM.Add.mss.34929/293]

PREVOTT, Miss, was born in Government House, Dominica, on 27 April 1803. [GM.73.594]

PRICE, GILBERT, from Tobago, died in Bath on 3 March 1807. [GM.77.381]

PRICE, THOMAS MACNAMARA ROSE, born 1847, eldest son of Lieutenant Governor Price, grandson of the late Sir Rose Price, died in Dominica on 16 April 1864. [GM.ns2.16.807]

PRIMROSE, JOHN, son of Reverend Dr Primrose in Prestonpans, the Deputy Treasury Officer, died in Kingston, St Vincent, on 19 September 1831. [AJ.4388]

PRINGLE, HALL, a stipendiary magistrate of the Windward District of Tobago from 1846 to 1853.

PRINGLE, JOHN, born 1771, master carpenter of the Ordnance Works in Dominica, died there in 1793. [EA.3146.118]

PRINGLE, KENNY, a carpenter in Tobago,witness to a deed in Shirwan, Tobago, 2 May 1792. [NRS.RD3.257.361]

PRINGLE, THOMAS, settled in St Paul's parish, Dominica, in July 1768. [TNA.CO142.31]

PRINGLE, WALTER, settled in St Paul's parish, Dominica, in July 1768. [TNA.CO142.31]

PRINN, JOHN, a Royal Engineers Clerk of Works, died in Dominica on 4 August 1853. [GM.ns.40.426]

PROUDFOOT, EDMUND, from Grenada, died in Martinique on 8 May 1794. [GM.64.671]

PULTENEY, DANIEL, born 1751, former Member of Parliament for Bramber, the Customs Officer of Dominica, Senior Fellow of King's College, Cambridge, died in 1811. [GM.81.194]

PURCELL, JAMES, constable in Rosseau, Trinidad in 1847. [DC.17.2.1847]

PURCELL, JOSEPH, in Grenada, probate, 1803, PCC. [TNA]

PURCELL, PATRICK JOSEPH, in Grenada, probate, 1807, PCC. [TNA]

PURSER, Dr WILLIAM ALLEN, born 1829 in Ireland, a doctor, musician and Moravian missionary, settled in Tobago in 1853, died 1895.

PYKE, WILLIAM, in Grenada, probate, 1808, PCC. [TNA]

PYM, J. E., son of J. Pym in London, the Provost Marshal of Grenada, died there on 17 October 1802. [GM.72.1161]

QUAST, JOHANNIS, a Dutch Reformed Church minister in Curacao from 1757

QUITELLE, ..., a creole from Martinique, a sloop-master. [SPAWI.1730.58]

RAE, JAMES, a minister in Grenada from 1888 to 1893. [F.7.667]

RAECX, EVERARD, in the service of the New West India Company in Curacao before 1728. [SPAWI.1729.684]

RAITT, ALEXANDER, of Bankmill, Aberdeen, died in St Lucia in 1817. [S.I.45]

THE PEOPLE OF THE WINDWARD ISLANDS, TRINIDAD AND TOBAGO, AND CURACAO, 1620-1860

RAMSAY, GEORGE, born 1805, son of Peter Ramsay and his wife Elizabeth Robertson, died in Trinidad on 20 May 1843. [Greyfriars gravestone, Perth]

RAMSAY, Miss, born 1791, only daughter of General Ramsay in the Leeward and Windward Islands, died in Port Royal, Martinique, on 5 May 1809. [GM.79.678]

RANKINE, DONALD, in Tobago, dead by 1822. [NRS.CS17.1.41.604]

RANKIN, WILLIAM, son of James Rankin in Hendon, Middlesex, died in Grenada on 27 December 1820. [GM.91.378]

RASVELT, WIGBOLDUS, a Dutch Reformed Church minister in Curacao from 1730 until his death in 1757. [NWIC.588.646]

RATEERE, JACOB, from Curacao to New York in 1699. [SPAWI.1699.680]

READING, JOHN, born 1734, a surgeon from London, emigrated via Plymouth aboard the Lovely Betsy bound for Dominica in March 1774. [TNA.T47.9-11]

REAY, JOHN, born in Dalmellington, died in Roseau, Dominica, on 2 April 1821. [BM.10.359][EEC.17214][S.4.246]

REDHEAD, ELLEN, daughter of George Redhead in Antigua, former Captain of the 3rd Guards Regiment, married James Athill, Lieutenant of the Royal Navy in London on 13 March 1850. [GM.ns33.657]

REDKNAP, EMILY, wife of Henry S. Redknap from Tobago, died in Twickenham on 8 March 1857. [GM.ns2/2.501]

REDWOOD, J. L., born 1766, from St Vincent, died 28 June 1807. [GM.77.593]

REED, LEONORA MATILDA, daughter of W. Reed in St Vincent, married W. Talbot Agar, only son of W. Agar, Queen's Counsel, in Lymington on 29 July 1843. [GM.ns20.428]

REES, EVAN, born 1774, from St Vincent, died in Llanidloes on 19 August 1855. [GM. ns54.443]

REID, ADAM, born 1795 in Aberdeen, died on Mount Desire, Carriacou on 21 February 1867. [S.7395]

REID, AGNES, widow of Alexander Scott Chalmers, died in Rutland Vale, St Vincent, on 23 February 1863. [AJ.25.3.1863]

REID, FRANCIS, born 1788, son of James Reid and his wife Ann Halliday in Dalton, Dumfries-shire, surgeon of the 35th Regiment of Foot, died in St Lucia on 5 April 1828. [Dalton gravestone]

REID, GEORGE, a labourer from Banff, a Jacobite banished to the Leeward Islands, liberated by the French and landed on Martinique in 1747. [TNA.SP36.102][P.3.266]

REID, JAMES, a labourer from Aberdeen or Angus, a Jacobite banished to the Leeward Islands, liberated by the French and landed on Martinique in 1747. [TNA.SP36.102][P.3.266]

REID, JOHN, seised of the cotton plantation called Bellair in Carriacou on 16 November 1772, a merchant in Carriacou in 1779. [NRS.CS16.1.175/179]; born 1732, 'late of Carriacou', died on 17 May 1815. [St Alphege's gravestone, Greenwich]

REID, MARIA, second daughter of Lieutenant Colonel Reid, Governor of the Windward Islands, married Lieutenant E. G. Hore, second son of Captain Hore of the Royal Navy, Pole Hore, Wexford, in Barbados on 17 June 1847. [GM.ns28.312]

REID, ROBERT, possibly from Aberdeen, an overseer in Carriacou, 1773. [PSAS.114.489]

THE PEOPLE OF THE WINDWARD ISLANDS, TRINIDAD AND TOBAGO, AND CURACAO, 1620-1860

REID, ROBERT, a planter of Machourere sugar estate, Dominica, 28 July 1804. [Caribbeana.3.309]

REID, WILLIAM, born 1813, son of David Reid and his wife Jen Baillie, died in Trinidad in 1843. [Brechin gravestone]

RHODES, Mr., from Barbados, died in Bath in October 1761. [GM.21.538]

RIALL, Major General, Governor of Grenada, married Miss Scarlett, eldest daughter of James Scarlett in Jamaica, in December 1819. [GM.89.635]

RICARDO, DANIEL ISRAEL, died in Curacao on 10 September 1749. [Beth Hain Cemetery, Curacao]

RICH, ANDREW, died on Mount Rich, Grenada, on 27 November 1779. [GMerc.3.]

RICHARD, COUSIN, born 1745, a gentleman from London, emigrated aboard the Proudfoot bound via Plymouth for Grenada in October 1774. [TNA.T47.9/11]

RICHARDSON, THOMAS, a gentleman from London, aboard the Darlington bound for Dominica in October 1775. [TNA.T47.9/11]

RICHARDSON, WILLIAM, from St Vincent, married Elizabeth Gardiner, daughter of David Gardiner of Kirktonhill, there on 7 October 1789. [GM.59.954]

RICHARDSON, HANNAH, widow of Anthony Richardson in Grenada, died in Welshpool on 3 February 1798. [GM.68.175]

RICHARDSON, WILLIAM, from St Vincent, married Elizabeth Gardiner, daughter of David Gardiner of Kirktonhill, there on 7 October 1789. [GM.59.954]

RIDDELL, JAMES, late in Grenada, was admitted as a burgess and guilds-brother of Ayr on 27 July 1776. [AyrBR]

RIDDELL, ROBERT, a farrier and horse doctor in Edinburgh, an indentured servant of James Hay of Lower Lalante Estate, Grenada, deed, 8 May 1792, witnessed by Hugh Rose from St George, Grenada. [NRS.RD3.256.57]

RIDDELL, THOMAS, born 1776, son of Thomas Riddell of Bessborough, Berwickshire, a Captain of the 14th Regiment, died in Trinidad on 16 September 1802. [Greyfriars gravestone]

RITCHIE, Reverend Dr DAVID, born 13 January 1753 in Perth, minister of St George, Grenada, later Rector of Roseau, Dominica, died there on 22 September 1801. [SM.64.181][FPA.319][EMA.52][GM.72.181]

RITCHIE, MARY, daughter of Charles Ritchie a merchant in Edinburgh, married Henry Cockburn minister of St Andrew's, Grenada, there on 22 August 1839. [SG.813]

RIVIERE, MAGDALEINE, in St Vincent in 1777. [JCTP.84.69/100]

ROBB, ELIZABETH, born 1712, a knitter from Aberdeen, a Jacobite banished to the Leeward Islands, liberated by the French and landed on Martinique in 1747. [TNA.SP36.102][P.3.274]

ROBB, THOMAS, married Elsie Cumming, daughter of Robert Cumming in Auldearn, in San Fernando, Trinidad, on 24 August 1852. [W.1361]

ROBE, JOHN, from Bristol, died in St Vincent on 16 November 1806. [GM.77.376]

ROBERTS, GEORGE, a surgeon, died in Marley, Grenada, on 9 January 1821. [AJ.3864]

ROBERTS, Mr., born 1754, a gentleman, via Plymouth aboard the Le Soy Planter bound for Dominica in 1774. [TNA.T47.9/11]

ROBERTSON, ALEXANDER KEITH, eldest son of Reverend George Hume Robertson in Ladykirk, Berwickshire, died in Kingston, St Vincent, on 24 February 1845. [AJ.5069][EEC.21155][W.547]

ROBERTSON, ISAAC, a mill carpenter on the Richmond Estate, St George's, Grenada, testament, 5 October 1791, Comm. Aberdeen. [NRS]

ROBERTSON, JOHN, born 24 November 1751 in Kincardine, Rain, son of Reverend Gilbert Robertson and his wife Christina Bayne, died in Tobago. [F.7.61]

ROBERTSON, JOHN, a minister in St Vincent, probate, 1776, PCC. [TNA]

ROBERTSON, JOHN, Judge of the Admiralty Court in Martinique, died in St Vincent in 1794. [GM.64.865]

ROBERTSON, WALTER, in Tobago, second son of Arthur Robertson, a surgeon in Old Meldrum, and his wife Katherine Stewart, a deed, subscribed in Grenada on 7 June 1771, witnesses were Alexander Symson in Grenada, and George Cracke, master of the Janet and Ann of Aberdeen. [NRS.RD3.238/2.23]

ROBERTSON, WALTER, in Tobago, probate 1789, PCC. [TNA]

ROBERTSON, WILLIAM, born 1727, a Jacobite prisoner banished to the Leeward Islands, liberated by the French and landed on Martinique in 1747. [P.3.280][TNA.SP36.102]

ROBERTSON, WILLIAM, born 1730, a labourer from Perth, a Jacobite prisoner banished to the Leeward Islands, liberated by the French and landed on Martinique in 1747. [P.3.280][TNA.SP36.102]

ROBERTSON and BELT, merchant in Curacao in 1812. [CGCA:11.12.1812]

ROBINSON, JOHN, born 1734, from Gosport, aboard the Aurora bound from Portsmouth for Dominica in October 1774, [TNA.T47.9-11]; from Dominica, died in Epsom, Surrey, on 6 July 1809. [GM.79.685]; in Dominica, probate, 1809, PCC. [TNA]

ROBINSON, JOHN, born 1759, a clerk, emigrated from London aboard the Westerhall bound for the Grenades in November 1774. [TNA.T47.9/11]

ROBINSON, WALTER, Lord Chief Justice of Tobago, aboard the Unity bound for Tobago, in July 1774. [TNA.T47.9-11]

ROBLEY, JOHN, President of Tobago, died in Golden Grove, Trinidad, on 3 November 1821. [GM.92.91]

ROBLEY, JOSEPH, born 1749, a planter in Tobago, returned from London aboard the Tobago Planter in February 1774. [TNA.T47.9-11]; in Tobago, probate, 1806, PCC. [TNA]

ROBLEY, SYBIL, daughter of John Robley in Trinidad, married Henry Pritchard of London, in Clifton on 7 April 1859. [GM.ns2/6.536]

ROCHE, JOSIAS, Captain of HMS Quebec died in St George, Grenada, on 25 April 1795. [St George gravestone, Grenada]

RODENBUSCH, LUCAS, Governor of Curacao in 1654.

RODGER, WILLIAM, an assistant surgeon in the Royal Navy, son of deacon James Rodger in Ayr, died in Grenada in October 1838. [SG.8.769]

ROEBUCK, ..., son of F. A. Disney Roebuck, a Captain of the 23rd Royal Welsh Fusiliers, was born in Trinidad on 7 October 1846. [GM.ns25.86]

ROGERS, MOSES, born 1746, a merchant from London, via Plymouth aboard the Lawrent bound for Dominica in January 1774. [TNA.T47.9-11]

ROLDAN, MARTIN, a Roman Catholic priest in Curacao in 1747

ROME, TRISTRAM, born 1773, son of John Rome and his wife Jean Cockpen, settled in Dominica before 1795, died there in 1797. [Dornock gravestone]

ROSE, JAMES, of St Vincent, late in Dundee, testaments, 1822, Comm. Brechin. [NRS]

ROSE, JOHN, jr., constable in St Patrick's, Dominica, 1847. [DC:27.2.1847]

ROSE, RODERICK, of Grenada, died in Norfolk, Virginia, on 13 October 1799. [GM.69.1087]

ROSS, DANIEL, born 177 in Ross-shire, a Jacobite prisoner banished to the Leeward Islands, liberated by the French and landed on Martinique in 1747. [P.3.286][TNA.SP36.102]

ROSS, DAVID R., 22 March 1797 in Rosstrevor, County Down, the Lieutenant Governor of Tobago, died there on 27 July 1851. [GM.ns36.542]

ROSS, JAMES, born 1727, a carpenter from Edinburgh, a Jacobite prisoner banished to the Leeward Islands, liberated by the French and landed on Martinique in 1747. [P.3.280][TNA.SP36.102]

ROSS, JOHN, a merchant late of Tobago, died at the Cove of Cork on 8 February 1781. [GM.4.78]

ROSS, JOHN, in Dominica, probate, 1787, PCC. [TNA]

ROSS, JOHN, born 1806, son of John Ross [1725-1782], a butcher in Aberdeen, and his wife Susannah Johnston [1724-1795], died in Tobago on 3 August 1826. [St Peter's, Spittal, gravestone]

ROSS, JOHN, born 1778, son of Alexander Ross [1737-1783] and his wife Margaret Udny [1732-1819], died in Clark's Court, Grenada, on 26 September 1833. [St Nicholas gravestone, Aberdeen]

ROSS, JOHN PEMBERTON, a barrister at law in St Vincent in 1823.

ROSS, ROBERT GEORGE, baptised 20 April 1787 in Lerwick, fourth son of Henry Ross, a writer, and his wife Janet Malcolmson, died in Tobago. [Zetland County Families, p221; Lerwick, 1893]

ROSS, WILLIAM, born 1711, a sailor from Edinburgh, a Jacobite prisoner banished to the Leeward Islands, liberated by the French and landed on Martinique in 1747. [P.3.290][TNA.SP36.102]

ROSS, THOMAS WILLIAM, son of Duncan Ross, a farmer in Rydnach, [1776-1824] and his wife Marjory McDonald [1779-1844], settled in St Vincent. [Kincardine, Strathspey, gravestone]

ROSS, WILLIAM, son of Alexander Ross in Aberdeen, died in St George, Grenada, on 10 October 1806. [AJ.3081]

ROSS, Miss, daughter of the late Peter Ross in Dominica, married Mr Adams in Newington, Surrey, in London on 18 July 1799. [GM.69.1189][EA.3711.55]

ROUDETT, ..., son of Benoit Roudett, was born in Dominica in August 1859. [DC.954]

ROUGEL, L. H., in Grenada, a deed, 1836. [NRS.RD5.545.495]

ROY, ANDREW, born 1845, died in St Vincent on 29 July 1877. [Straiton gravestone, Ayrshire]

RUDDACH, CHARLES, late of Tobago, brother of Thomas Ruddach a merchant in Tobago, a sasine, 27 August 1806. [NRS.RS.Orkney.670]

RUDDACH, THOMAS, son of Reverend Alexander Ruddach in Kirkwall, sasines, 7 September 1791 and 27 August 1806, [NRS.RS.ORKNEY.252/676][NLS.ms5028/40]; a merchant in Tobago, probate, 1800, PCC. [TNA]

RUSSEL, MARY, wife of John I. I. Alexander in St Lucia, relict of Robert Cullen in Scotland, died in St Lucia on 10 February 1818. [AJ.3672]

RUSSELL, THOMAS, born 1781, son of Thomas Russell of Rathen and his wife Anna Innes, a midshipman, died in Martinique in July 1794. [Banff gravestone]

RUSSELL, THOMAS, born 1817, son of John Russell and his wife Jane Cuthbertson in Lanark, a book-binder, died in Trinidad on 28 May 1838. [Lanark gravestone]

RUSSELL, WILLIAM, a planter in Tobago, died 1790. [NRS.GD44.34.46.1]

RUTHERFORD, JAMES, a planter in Grenada, a deed, 6 October 1796, witnesses were Richard Landreath, a planter in Grenada, and George Paterson, a physician in Grenada, [NRS.RD3.276.249]

RYEBURN, JOHN, in St George, Grenada, co-owner of the Pomona of Glasgow, and of the Alfred of Glasgow in 1798, and of the Nancy of Greenock in 1805. [NRS.CE60.11.5.7.1.108; 8.83]

SABAZAN, JOSEPH, born 1781, died on Black Bay Estate, Grenada, on 28 November 1820. [GM.91.185]

SAINT AMOUR, Sieur HENRY, in Martinique in 1688. [SPAWI.1688.1718i]

SAINT MARTIN, ..., Governor of St Lucia in 1719. [SPAWI.1719.384/404/411/422/439/469/505]

SALTER, WILLIAM, born 1796, from Exeter, Customs Landing Surveyor, died in St Lucia on 30 September 1839. [GM.ns13.333]

SAMUEL, GEORGE, born 1729, a book-binder from Edinburgh, a Jacobite prisoner banished to the Leeward Islands, liberated by the French and landed on Martinique in 1747. [P.3.280][TNA.SP36.102]

SAMUEL, SAMUEL, a merchant in Trinidad, 1843. [PSG.1806]

SANBATCH, JOHN, born 1761, from London aboard the Marquis of Rockingham bound for the Grenades in November 1774. [TNA.T47.9/11]

SANDERSON, EDWARD DYER, born 1810, Chief Justice of Tobago 1853, died there on 20 April 1861. [GM.ns2/10.705][TNA.CO225.25.31]

SANG, WILLIAM, son of William Sang a baker in Aberdeen, settled in Tobago before 1828. [St Nicholas gravestone, Aberdeen]; late of Tobago, died in Grove, Aberdeen, on 8 July 1842. [AJ.4933]

SANGSTER, PATRICK, eldest son of John Sangster in Widewalls, Orkney, died in Grenada in 1817. [S.I.32]

SASLAS, MOSES, died in Curacao on 20 November 1799. [Beth Hain Cemetery, Curacao]

SASSO, ARON, manager of Gabriel Pinedo's plantation of Wacau in Curacao in 1792. [NWIC.566.556]

SAURES, ISAAC, born 1746, a merchant from Curacao, was naturalised in South Carolina on 13 September 1808. [NARA.M1183/1]

SAURES, JACOB, born 1774, a merchant from Curacao, was naturalised in South Carolina on 13 September 1808. [NARA.M1183/1]

SCAMBLE, JOHN, born 1809, son of George Scamble, died in Trinidad on 27 July 1828. [Wigtown gravestone]

SCHABEL, MIGUEL ALEXIS, born in Bohemia, a Jesuit priest, in Curacao from 1704 to 1713.

SCHINK, Father, a Dutch Franciscan priest on Curacao in 1778, the Apostolic Prefect there in 1787.

SCOTLAND, Reverend JOHN, of St John's College, Oxford, second son of John Scotland the Chief Judge in Trinidad, married Elizabeth Snow Heath, second daughter of Thomas Heath, in Putney on 10 January 1849. [GM.ns31.312]

SCOTT, ALEXANDER, a Councillor, died in Grenada on 1 June 1806. [GM.76.978]; in Grenada, probate, 1807, PCC. [TNA]

SCOTT, ANDREW, an attorney, youngest son of Andrew Scott of Knockbay, Grange, Banffshire, died on Westerhall Estate, Grenada, on 17 September 1844. [AJ.5054]

SCOTT, AUGUSTA MARY, wife of Frederick John Scott, died in Port of Spain, Trinidad, on 18 January 1862. [S.2082][EEC.23685]

SCOTT, GEORGE, in Grenada, probate, 1768, PCC. [TNA]

SCOTT, GEORGE, Governor of Dominica, died in 1768. [GM.38.47]

SCOTT, HELEN, born 1844, from Edinburgh, wife of William Miller on Santa Margarita Estate, Trinidad, died on 6 January 1870. [S.8273]

SCOTT, HENRY ELLIOT, born 1847, late of the Electric Tile Company of Edinburgh, died in Trinidad on 30 November 1869. [S.8247]

SCOTT, JOHN, born 1730, a herd from Atholl, a Jacobite prisoner who was banished to the Leeward Islands, liberated by the French and landed on Martinique in 1747.[TNA.SP36.102]

SCOTT, JOSEPH, President of the Legislative Council of Tobago 1838. [Parliamentary Papers, 1839]

SCOTT, WILLIAM, born 1824, son of Robert Scott and his wife Margaret McKechnie in Perth, died in Trinidad on 16 April 1845. [Greyfriars gravestone, Perth]

SCOTT, Mrs, widow of Michael Scott in Grenada, married the Count de la Basecque, in Artois, France, in November 1792. [GM.84.697]

SEATON, ALEXANDER, born 1752, a clerk from Scotland, emigrated via London aboard the Industry bound for the Grenades in April 1774. [TNA.T47.9-11]

SELLAR, DAVID, a planter in Tobago, will, 18 October 1810. [NRS.RD3.336.135]

SELS, JOOST, Rear Admiral, died in Curacao in September 1759.

SEMPLE, JOHN W., an advocate, died in Castries, St Lucia, in 1842. [EEC.20530]

SENIOR, ESTHER, died 1714 in Curacao. [Curacao gravestone]

SENIOR, ISAAC HAIM, a merchant in Curacao, died 1726. [Curacao gravestone]

SETON, CHARLOTTE, daughter of Governor Seton of St Vincent, married Arthur Leith, a Captain of the 69th Regiment in the Caribees on 21 June 1791. [GM.61.871]; on 5 October 1807, she, then a widow, married Captain Henry Evans. [GM.77.976]

SETON, GEORGE, second son of Governor Seton, died in St Vincent on 21 August 1795. [GM.65.968]; probate, 1796, PCC. [TNA]

SETON, JAMES, jr., married Mrs Mackay, from St Vincent, in Bishop
Auckland on 1 January 1799. [GM.69.77]

SHAPLEY, Reverend J. CONGDON, in Carriacou, Grenada, married
Mary Jane Milne, youngest daughter of A. G. Milne in Eltham, Kent,
on 13 June 1844. [GM.na22.202]

SHARPE, EDWARD, warden of Rosseau, Dominica, in 1840.
[DC27.2.1847]

SHARPE, FRANCES, born 1760, widow of John MacArthur Sharpe the
Solicitor General of Grenada, and sister of Sir Peter Payne, died in
Bedford on 9 February 1844. [GM.ns21.444]

SHARPE, GEORGE, in St Vincent, married C. Payne, second daughter
of Sr Gillies Payne of Tempsford, Bedfordshire, in 1788.
[GM.58.1026]; probate, 1807, PCC. [TNA]

SHARPE, GEORGE HENRY, born 1804, from St Vincent, died in
Bedford on 25 October 1853. [GM.ns40.652]

SHARPE, LAURA, youngest daughter of Henry Edward Sharpe the
Chief Justice of St Vincent, married Charles Lionel John Fitzgerald, a
Lieutenant of the 1st West Indian Regiment, eldest son of Lieutenant
Colonel Fitzgerald of the Royal Artillery, in St George, St Vincent, on
12 March 1863. [GM.ns.2/14.781]

SHARPE, MARIA, eldest daughter of John Sharpe the Attorney
General of Grenada, married Reverend L., in Tempsford,
Bedfordshire, in 1812. [GM.82.288]

SHARP, WILLIAM, born 1729, a labourer from Aberdeen, a Jacobite
prisoner banished to the Leeward Islands, liberated by the French
and landed on Martinique in 1747. [TNA.SP36.102]

SHAW, WILLIAM, born 1831, son of Alexander Shaw [1790-1859]. Settled in Grenada, died in Carriacou on 9 October 1864. [Crathie gravestone]

SHERGOLD, WILLIAM WHITMORE, died in St Vincent on 21 August 1804. [GM.74.1168]

SHERIFF, ALEXANDER, a planter in Dominica, father of Francis and Judith, a landowner in Nevis, and guardian of Thomas Sheriff of 'Traverseburgh' in Scotland, 11 January 1780. [Dominica Book of Wills, number 195]

SHIPLEY, Sir CHARLES, born 1757, Governor of Grenada, died there on 30 November 1815. [GM.86.276]

SIEVEWRIGHT, COLIN, MD, born 1792, died in Trinidad on 16 January 1818. [AJ.3670]

SILVER, DAVID, MA, a minister in Grenada from 1897 to 1902, died 30 November 1921. [F.7.667]

SIM, JAMES, born 11 November 1759 in Banff, husband of Elizabeth McKilligan [1761-1826], settled in St Vincent, died 27 May 1825. [Banff gravestone]

SIMMONS, JACOB, in Trinidad, testament, 3 December 1823, Comm. Edinburgh. [NRS]

SIMPSON, ALEXANDER, a Baron of the Exchequer in Grenada, was granted the lands of Auchenleck on 23 February 1771. [NRS.RGS.111.140]

SIMPSON, JAMES, in Tobago, was admitted as a burgess of Banff in 1773. [Banff Burgess Roll]

SIMPSON, JAMES, a merchant from Glasgow, in Grenada in 1776, [NLS.Acc.8793.13]; there in 1780. [NRS.CS16.1.177]

SIMPSON, JOHN, the naval officer of St Vincent in 1772. [NRS.CS16.1.151.48]

SIMPSON, JOSEPH, in Grenada in 1800. [NRS.S/H.1800]

SIMPSON, JOSEPH, warden of St Joseph's parish, Dominica, 1847. [DC27.2.1847]

SIMPSON, WILLIAM, deceased by 1812, in Grenada, [NRS.RD5.59.545]

SINCLAIR, ARCHIBALD, born 1781, eldest son of Alexander Sinclair in Kilchamaig, Argyll, died at Mount Irvine, Tobago, on 11 September 1823. [EEC.17549][Cladh Nicheil gravestone, Kintyre]

SINCLAIR, DONALD, born 1817, late overseer in Grenada, died in Auchenalate, Argyll, on 1 July 1847. [Glendaruel gravestone]

SINCLAIR, WILLIAM, the Paymaster of Dominica, married Augusta Brush, daughter of John Brush, in Dominica in 1794. [EA.3208.205]; in Dominica, probate, 1798, PCC. [TNA]

SINCLAIR, WILLIAM, in St Vincent, 1844. [NRS.S/H.1844]

SISSON, MARY, wife of A Sisson, third daughter of T Neale in Reigate, Surrey, died in Rosseau, Dominica, on 24 August 1841. [GM.ns16.558]

SLADDEN, WALTER, an overseer on Orange Valley Estate, Tobago, in 1845.

SLOSS, GILBERT, an iron-monger from Ayr, died in St Vincent on 7 February 1851. [W.1200]

SMALL, ALEXANDER, in St Vincent, a bond in favour of William Small in St Vincent, a bond, 1 April 1813. [NRS.RD5.173.696]

SMART, JOHN, second son of …. Smart in Marykirk, Kincardineshire, died in Tobago on 21 December 1817. [AJ.3658]

SMITH, CHARLES, a merchant in Curacao, died in Portsmouth on 16 September 1809. [GM.79.894]

SMITH, CHARLOTTE, daughter of Robert Smith the Speaker of the Assembly of Tobago, married Charles Simpson Hanson from Constantinople, in Woodford, Essex, in September 1829. [GM.99.270]

SMITH, JAMES, born 1772, a merchant in Grenada, died in St Lucia on 23 April 1799. [AJ.2688]

SMITH, JOHN, born 1726, a goldsmith from Aberdeen, a Jacobite prisoner banished to the Leeward Islands, liberated by a French privateer and landed in Martinique in 1747. [TNA.SP36.102]

SMITH, JOHN, born 1734, a planter, from London bound for the Grenades aboard the Grenada Galley in June 1774. [TNA.T47.9-11]

SMITH, Dr JOHN, in St Vincent, dead by 1816. [NRS.S/H]

SMITH, Dr THOMAS, born 1763 in Largo, Fife, '57 years in the West Indies, a survivor of the Carib Wars', died in St Vincent on 3 January 1840. [FH.3.1.1840]

SMITH, WILLIAM, born 1738, a gentleman, via Plymouth aboard the Le Soy Planter bound for Dominica in 1774. [TNA.T47.9/11]

SMITH, WILLIAM, in Grenada, married Miss Johnstone from Liverpool, on 5 November 1792. [GM.62.1054]

SMITH, WILLIAM, in St Vincent in 1856. [NRS.S/H.1856]

SMYTH, FRANCIS, in St Vincent, probate, 1807, PCC. [TNA]

SNAGG, ANNE ISABELLA, daughter of W. Snagg in St Vincent, married Reverend H. S. Pollard, second son of R. B. Pollard in Brompton, in London on 15 May 1838. [GM.ns10.92]

SNELL, Dr JAMES, born 1794, died at Peter's Hope, St Vincent, on 6 July 1850. [St Vincent gravestone][GM.ns34.331]

SOMERVILLE, PETER, born 1732, a shoemaker, a Jacobite prisoner banished to the Leeward Islands, liberated by the French and landed on Martinique in 1747. [TNA.SP36.102][P.3.326]

SORHANDE, NICHOLAS, constable in St Patrick's, Dominica, 1847. [DC: 27.2.1847]

SPAN, HARRIET, wife of Samuel Span in Bristol, died in Trinidad on 3 November 1809. [GM.79.1236]

SPAN, JOHN, a merchant from Bristol, married Dorothea Munro, daughter of Hugh Munro in Carriacou, in Grenada on 2 November 1796. [GM.66.965]

SPAN, SAMUEL, in St Vincent, probate, 1811, PCC. [TNA]

SPEARS, WILLIAM, died in St Lucia on 2 May 1794. [GM.64.767]

SPEGHT, PHILIP, a Dutch Reformed minister in Curacao from 1668 to 1679.

SPENCE, ALEXANDER, a minister in St Vincent from 1841. [F.7.671]

SPIER, THOMAS THORNEVILLE, died in St Vincent on 7 November 1806. [GM.77.277]

SPOTTISWOODE, THOMSON, from Tobago, died in Falmouth on 24 October 1796. [GM.66.1059]

STAFFORD, FREDERICK, born 1822, seventh son of Brabazon Stafford in Dublin, died in Port of Spain, Trinidad, on 5 November 1857. [GM.ns2/4.112]

STALKER, DUNCAN, from Argyll, a planter in Tobago, a will, 8 May 1796. [NRS.RD4.263.1035], in Kintyre, testament, 1798, Comm. Argyll. [NRS]; formerly in Tobago, later in Killean, Argyll, an edict of executry in 1798. [NRS.CC2.8.102.7]

STANDIFORD, Mrs, wife of English Standiford, died in Port Royal, Martinique, on 18 October 1800. [GM.71.275]

STARRAT, ROBERT, sometime in Carriacou, Grenada, a sasine, 1829. [NRS.RS54.5279]

STEDMAN, HUNTER, born in Edinburgh on 20 December 1812, moved to the West Indies in 1839, settled in Philadelphia in 1849, a wine merchant, returned to the West Indies in 1890, died in Rosseau, Dominica, on 2 September 1900. [AP.333]

STEDMAN, WILLIAM, a merchant in Market Square, Rosseau, Dominica, in 1859. [DC.954]

STEEL, Captain HENRY, born 1715 in South Queensferry, died in Grenada in 1774. [South Queensferry gravestone]

STEEL, THOMAS, son of Robert Steel a writer in Lanark, died in Tobago in 1801. [AJ.2807]

STEELE, Mrs, daughter of Robert Burke in Prospect Lota, County Cork, married George Hyde, in St Vincent on 7 October 1820. [GM.90.562].

STEPHENS, CATHERINE, youngest daughter of Colonel Stephens in St Lucia, married Reverend W. J. Heale, in Berrow, Worcestershire, on 28 November 1837. [GM.ns9.88]

STEPHEN, GEORGE, in Grand Pauvre, Diamond Estate, Grenada, in 1785. [NRS.GD58.1.16.426]

STEPHEN, Miss, daughter of G. Stephen in Grenada, married Rear Admiral Sir David Milne on 28 November 1819. [GM.89.563]

STEPHENSON, Dr WILLIAM, a physician on the Waltham Estate, Grenada, in 1803. [NRS.GD267.5.11.1]

STEUART, JAMES HOPE, born in Gillensbie on 20 December 1828, son of James Hope Steuart and his wife Helen Bell, died in Port of Spain, Trinidad, on 18 March 1859. [Dryfesdale gravestone]

STEVEN, ALEXANDER, son of Alexander Steven late in Tobago, was educated at King's College, Aberdeen, a sasine, 1790. [KCA.2.37][NRS.RS.Banff.336]

STEVENS, GEORGE, born 1834, son of Mrs Stevens in Hoxton, a merchant, died in Castries, St Lucia, on 18 September 1852. [GM.ns38.656]

STEVENS, HENRY, born 1833, son of Mrs Stevens in Hoxton, a merchant, died in Castries, St Lucia, on 18 September 1852. [GM.ns38.656]

STEVENS, JOHN, in Trinidad, a deed, 1 December 1826. [NRS.RD5.347/767]

STEVEN, WILLIAM, from Falkirk, died in San Fernando, Trinidad, on 25 September 1840. [W.97]

STEVENSON, ARCHIBALD, in Edward Street, Port of Spain, Trinidad, in 1843. [PSG.1806]

STEVENSON, JAMES, died in Grenada on 24 June 2795. [GM.65.879]

STEVENSON, Dr WILLIAM, in Grenada, 1803. [NRS.NRAS.0682; GD267.5.11]

STEWART, ALEXANDER, in Dominica, a bond, 25 April 1774. [NRS.RD4.215.486]

STEWART, ARCHIBALD, a planter in Dominica, died in 1777, testament, 1798, Comm. Edinburgh. [NRS]

STEWART, ARCHIBALD, a merchant in Rotterdam, later in Tobago by 1778. [NRS.CS16.1.173.313]

STEWART, CHARLES DOUGLAS, born 1804, a barrister, died in St Vincent in December 1864. [St Vincent gravestone]

STEWART, DANIEL, a surgeon in Dominica, married Jean Murray, in Canongait, Edinburgh, on 17 August 1777, [CMR]; services of heirs, 1787, [NRS]; father of Daniel Stewart in Petersburg, Virginia, a deed, 1805. [NRS.RD3.308.595]

STEWART, DAVID, of Garth, a Major General, later Governor of St Lucia, died in December 1829. [NRS.GD2.147]

STEWART, ESTHER NESS, born 1815, died in Williams Villa, Trinidad, on 21 December 1844. [New Calton gravestone, Edinburgh]

STEWART, HOUSTON, a planter on Roxburgh Estate, Tobago, in 1836. [TNA.T71.1572]

STEWART, JAMES, late in Grenada, died in Hart Street, Edinburgh, on 17 December 1819. [S.4.154]

STEWART, JAMES, from Dougalston, died in Grenada on 1 September 1852. [W.1367]

STEWART, JANE, widow of David Haldane, in Grenada, 1854. [NRS.S/H.1854]

STEWART, Mrs JEAN, daughter of William Murray a merchant in Edinburgh, wife of Daniel Stewart a surgeon in Dominica, a deed, 13 January 1778. [NRS.RD4.223.1.624]

STEWART, JOHN, born 1729, a labourer in Aberdeen, a Jacobite prisoner banished to the Leeward Islands, liberated by the French and landed on Martinique in 1747. [TNA.SP36.102][P.3.346]

STEWART, JOHN, born 1730, a labourer from Perthshire, a Jacobite prisoner banished to the Leeward Islands, liberated by the French and landed on Martinique in 1747. [TNA.SP36.102][P.3.346]

STEWART, JOHN, of Garth, Perthshire, died in Garth, Trinidad, on 28 March 1830. [S.1079]

STEWART, Mrs MATILDA, born 1804, died 19 December 1841. [St Vincent gravestone]

STEWART, ROBERT, a Lieutenant of the 61st Regiment, son of James Stewart of Urrard, Perthshire, died in Martinique on 28 June 1795. [CM.11597]

STEWART, WILLIAM, in Grenada, probate, 1777, PCC. [TNA]

STEWART, WILLIAM, late in Grenada, now in Inverugie, 4 July 1818. [NRS.RGS.157.23.52]

STEWART, Mrs, from St Vincent, died in London on 23 August 1820. [GM.90.283]

STEWART, Mrs, wife of Dr Alexander Stewart, died in Dominica on 11 May 1844. [GM.ns22.110]

STEWART-MCKENZIE, FRANCIS PELHAM, born 1820, second son of James Alexander Stewart-McKenzie, a Lieutenant in the Highland

Light Infantry and Fort Adjutant of Grenada, died on 21 December 1844. [St George gravestone, Grenada]

STIRLING, ARCHIBALD, was educated at Edinburgh University, minister of the united parishes of St Patrick's and St Andrew's in Grenada from1846 to 1851. [F.7.667]

STIRLING, NICOLAUS HOUTSCHILT, from Curacao, graduated from Leiden University in 1772. [University of Leiden, Holland]

STIRLING, Sir SAMUEL, a planter at King's Bay, Tobago, in 1836. [TNA.T71.1572]

STIVEN, REBECCA, daughter of Alexander Stiven in Tobago, married J. C. Johnstone of the Theatre Royal of Edinburgh, in Aberdeen in 1801. [GM.71.1050]

STODDART, GEORGE DOUGLAS, a planter on Calderhall Estate, Tobago, in 1836. [TNA.T71.1572]

STOPPEL, Father JOHANNES, a priest in Curacao in 1805.

STRACHAN, ROBERT, born 1777, a shipwright, died in St Vincent in 1805. [Howff gravestone, Dundee]

STRACHAN, SIMPSON, died in Mortendue, Grenada, on 25 October 1801. [GM.71.83]; in Grenada, probate, 1803, PCC. [TNA]

STRANG, JANET, daughter of Walter Strang in Edinburgh, married Reverend George Mitchell, in St George, Grenada, in 1862. [S.2126][AJ.5963]

STRUTH, CHARLES, son of Sir W. Struth, in St Vincent, died in New York in 1834. [GM.104.671]

STRUTH, Reverend NATHANIEL, born 1793, Speaker of the House of Assembly in St Vincent, died 30 January 1847. [St Vincent gravestone]

STUART, ALEXANDER, MD, born 1735, died in Grenada in August 1797. [GM.67.1069]

STUART, HENRY, in St George, Grenada, settled in Tobago in 1771. [NRS.GD225.box31, bundle 12]

STUART, JAMES, born 1778, settled in Grenada, died 17 December 1819. [Restalrig burial register, Edinburgh]

STUART, WILLIAM, born 1771 in Inverugie, Moray, died in Morne Delice, Grenada, on 21 August 1845. [AJ.5099]

STURROCK, JAMES, a merchant in Tobago, son of James Sturrock [1707-1765] and his wife Isabel Mudie [1712-1780]. [Arbirlot gravestone, Angus]

STUYLING, WILLEM, a planter in Curacao in 1766. [OAC.900.18]

STUYVESCANT, PIETER, Governor of Curacao in 1644.

SUTER, COLQUHOUN, sixth son of James Suter in Rothes, died in Kingston, St Vincent, on 29 September 1838. [AJ.4743]

SUTER, JAMES, born 1791, eldest son of Thomas Suter the sheriff clerk of Ross, died in Grenada in 1813. [AJ.3432]

SUTHERLAND, ADAM, born 1691, a labourer from Sutherland, a Jacobite prisoner banished to the Leeward Islands, liberated by the French and landed on Martinique in 1747. [TNA.SP36.102][P.3.358]

SUTHERLAND, JAMES, from St Vincent, died in Elgin, Moray, on 8 November 1841. [AJ.4898]

SUTHERLAND, ROBERT, born in Dunrobin in 1776, son of Robert Sutherland and is wife Elizabeth Baillie, to St Vincent in 1796, returned in 1817, of Millmount, Ross-shire, died 31 October 1828 in Hastings. [NRS.RS54.PR16.228; 1910] [GM.98.476][AJ.4218]

SUTHERLAND, ROBERT, born 1805 in Ross-shire, son of George Sackville Sutherland [1770-1812] and his wife Jean Mackay [1772-1858], settled in St Vincent in 1821, a stipendiary magistrate, married Georgina Cumming, parents of Robert Sutherland [1840-1887], died in London on 7 March 1883. [Kensington death register, 1883; 224]

SYBRANTSDOCHTER JELLETGE, from Curacao to the New Netherlands in 1640s. [NNC.57]

SYMON, JAMES, born 1791, a mason, died in Tobago on 5 July 1822. [Chapel Yard gravestone, Inverness]

SYMPSON, ALEXANDER, a land grant in St Andrew parish, Dominica in February 1768. [NRS.GD126/4]

TALON, GEORGE, born 1849, son of Reverend T. K. Talon, 2 Bellevue Terrace, Edinburgh, died in Trinidad on 29 July 1869. [S.8136]

TAUREAU, GABRIEL, in Dominica in 1772. [JCTP.1772.319]

TAYLOR, Dr ALEXANDER, a merchant in Grenada in 1776. [NLS.Acc.8793]

TAYLOR, DAVID, born 1787, son of John Taylor, a miller, and his wife Mary Mill, died in St Vincent in February 1822. [Fettercairn gravestone, Kincardineshire]

TAYLOR, GEORGE, son of James Taylor of Moorfield [1790-1861], died in St Vincent aged 23. [Kilmarnock gravestone, Ayrshire]

TAYLOR, JAMES, born 1799, son of Robert Taylor a merchant in Barrhead, a civil engineer who died in Trinidad on 28 January 1824. [Arthurlie gravestone]

TAYNTON, Mrs, widow of Nathaniel Taynton the Attorney General of Grenada, in Carriacou on 31 July 1813. [G.M., 83.620]

TEN OEVER, THEODORUS, a Roman Catholic priest in Curacao from 1759.

THAIN, ISOBEL, in Grenada, testament, 1869, Edinburgh. [NRS.SC70.1.145.561]

THAILOUIS, AUGUSTIN, a solicitor and notary public in Port of Spain, Trinidad, 1846. [TS:1.1.1846]

THOM, ROBERT, born 1731, a labourer from Angus, a Jacobite prisoner banished to the Leeward Islands, liberated by the French and landed on Martinique in 1747. [TNA.SP36.102][P.3.370]

THOMAS, CHARLES, born 1751, a clerk from Westminster, from London aboard the Tobago Planter bound for Tobago in February 1774. [TNA.T47.9-11]

THOMAS, JAMES, from London bound for the Grenades aboard the Grenada Galley in June 1774. [TNA.T47.9-11]

THOMAS, ROBERT, from Elie, Fife, married Elisabeth Atwell, widow of Samuel Hicks, born in Nevis, in Curacao on 7 March 1719. [Curacao Marriage Register]

THOMAS, ROBERT, formerly a merchant in Grenada, died in Liverpool in 1801. [GM.71.89]

THOMSON, A., in Grenada, a letter, 1798. [EUL.Laing.II.509]

THOMSON, ANDREW, a Captain of the Second West India Regiment, only son of James Thomson a baker in Edinburgh, died in Trinidad on 15 December 1800. [GM.71.275]

THOMSON, GEORGE, born in Ellon, Aberdeenshire, emigrated in 1843, died in Fairfield, Tobago, on 24 November 1846. [AJ.5169]

THOMPSON, JAMES, born 1726, a gardener from Perthshire, a Jacobite prisoner banished to the Leeward Islands, liberated by the French and landed on Martinique in 1747. [TNA.SP36.102][P.3.372]

THOMSON, JAMES, a staff assistant surgeon, died in Trinidad on 7 August 1828. [AJ.4218]

THOMSON, JOHN, from Banffshire, a Jacobite prisoner banished to the Leeward Islands, liberated by the French and landed on Martinique in 1747. [TNA.SP36.102][P.3.372]

THOMSON, MARGARET, daughter of Secretary Thomson of the Excise in Scotland, widow of James Bruce the Governor of Dominica, died in Roseau, Dominica, on 19 July 1817. [S.I.40.17]

THOMSON, WILLIAM, born 1707, a labourer from Kingoldrum, Angus, a Jacobite prisoner banished to the Leeward Islands, liberated by the French and landed on Martinique in 1747. [TNA.SP36.102][P.3.372]

THORNLEY, MONTAGUE, a Lieutenant of the Royal West India Rangers, died in St Lucia in April 1807. [GM.77.682]

THORNTON, GODFREY, in Dominica, probate, 1805, PCC. [TNA]

THORNTON, JOHN, Clerk to the Legislative Council of Tobago 1838. [Parliamentary Papers, 1839]

TINNE, PHILIP FREDERICK, the Secretary of Dominica, married Miss Rose, daughter of William Rose of Mountcoffer, at the Chateau Margo on 28 April 1806. [SM.68.564]

TITRE, GEORGE, in Dominica in 1773. [JCTP.1773.334]

TITRE, LEWIS JOSEPH, in Dominica in 1773. [JCTP.1773.334]

TODD, JAMES, born 23 February 1809, fourth son of John Todd, died in Belmont, Grenada, on 18 August 1853. [Kirkmaiden gravestone, Wigtownshire]

TODD, JAMES REEVES, MD, born 1840, medical officer of St John and St Marks, died in Charlottetown, Grenada, on 4 August 1867. [S.7511]

TODD, MELCHIOR GARNER, from St Lucia, married Marianne Emilia Frances Pryce, eldest daughter of Henry Pryce a Captain of the Royal Navy, in Clifton on 7 October 1845. [GM.ns24.650]; Melchior a former Councillor, died in Castries, St Lucia on 20 September 1866. [GM.ns3/2.698]; his son was born on Union Estate, St Lucia, on 18 May 1847. [GM.ns28.198]

TOOK ANN, born 1753, a servant, aboard the Greyhound at Plymouth bound for Dominica in December 1773. [TNA.T47.9/11]

TOVEY, COPLAND, son of Captain Tovey of the 5th Scots Regiment of Militia, died in Dominica on 21 August 1801. [GC.1582]

TRAILL, GEORGE, born in Laby, Sanday, Orkney, on 25 April 1746, son of Reverend Thomas Traill of Hobbister, and his wife Sibella Grant, died in Grenada in 1774. [F.7.264]

TRAILL, THOMAS, born 1720, settled in Dominica, died in July 1763. [St Andrews gravestone, Fife]

TRAILL, THOMAS, born in Laby, Sanday, Orkney, on 16 April 1749, son of Reverend Thomas Traill of Hobbister, and his wife Sibella Grant, died in St Vincent. [F.7.264]

TRAILL, WALTER, in Dominica from 1807 to 1815. [NRS.GD126.box 8]

TRAILL, WILLIAM, in Dominica, son of John Traill late tenant farmer in Strathkinness, Fife, and his first wife Isabel Stewart, a deed, 28 November 1793. [NRS.SC20.36.16]

TRAN, HUGH, son of Arthur Tran in Glasgow, settled in St Kitts in 1767, a merchant there, 1779, 1782, later in Dominica by 1783. [NRS.CS16.1.174; CS17.1.1/59/182; 2/247]; on 3 June1768, he, a merchant in Glasgow and St Kitts, became heir to his mother Elizabeth Warden, services of heirs, 1768. [NRS.B64.1.9.134/9]; a deed, in Grenada, 23 December 1771. [NRS.RD2.224/2.650]

TRAVERSIER, MICHAEL, in Dominica in 1772. [JCTP.79.8]

TREMBLANT, ..., in St Vincent in 1728. [SPAWI.1730.260.vii]

TREW, ANN, wife of Reverend J. M. Trew from St Thomas in the East, Jamaica, died in Grenada on 29 March 1842. [GM.ns18.223]

TREW, FANNY, born 1823, eldest daughter of Reverend J. M. Trew from St Thomas in the East, Jamaica, died in Grenada on 24 March 1842. [GM.ns18.223]

TREW, SOPHIA, daughter of Reverend J. M. Trew from St Thomas in the East, Jamaica, died in Grenada on 24 February 1842. [GM.ns18.223]

TROOP, JOHN, born 1727, a gardener from Stirling, a Jacobite prisoner banished to the Leeward Islands, liberated by the French and landed on Martinique in 1747. [TNA.SP36.102][P.3.378]

TROTTER, JOHN, died in Dominica on 12 February 1809. [SM.71.318]; testament, 2 November 1825, Comm. Edinburgh. [NRS]

TROUP, JONATHAN, son of Mathew Troup in Aberdeen, graduated MA from Marischal College in 1786, emigrated via London aboard the Duchess of Portland bound for Dominica in 1788, a surgeon there, died in Aberdeen after 1798. [NRS.NRAS.0486.2070][UAL.ms2070]

TUCKETT, J. W., from St Vincent, married Miss Twigg from London on 15 August 1803. [GM.73.985]

TULLOCH, HENRY BOWYER, Colonial Secretary of Dominica, second son of Lieutenant Colonel Tulloch of the Royal Artillery, died in Dominica on 12 July 1823. [GM.93.647][BM.14.624]

TULLOH, MARGARET ISABELLA, born 1804, wife of Lieutenant Alexander Tulloh of the Royal Artillery, daughter of William Bremner the President of Dominica, died there on 11 September 1826. [GM.96.574]

TURNBULL, ALEXANDER, died in Curacao in 1806. [AJ.3097]

TURNBULL, ALEXANDER, in Grenada, probate, 1809, PCC. [TNA]

TURNBULL, GORDON, a planter in Grenada, an inventory, 20 October 1809, Comm. Edinburgh. [NRS]

TURNBULL, STEWART, & Co., merchants, Marie Square, Port of Spain, Trinidad, 1846. [TS:1.1.1846]

TURNER, JOHN, born 1772, second son of John Turner of Turnerhall, died in Carriacou near Grenada on 3 June 1773. [AJ.2381]

TURNER, JOHN, fourth son of John Turner of Turnerhall and his wife Elizabeth Urquhart, died in Grenada on 2 June 1792. [TOF.554]

TURNER, ROBERT NICHOLSON, born 1808, son of Captain Robert Turner of the Royal Engineers, from Kelso, Roxburghshire, died in Tobago on 17 November 1840. [EEC.20172]

TWIGG, Miss, from London, married J. W. Tuckett, in St Vincent on 15 August 1803. [GM.73.985]

TYDDESLEY, THOMAS, born 1776 in Friery, Isle of Man, died on passage from St Vincent aboard the Elizabeth in 1798. [GM.68.814]

UDNEY, JOHN, in Grenada, probate, 1804, PCC. [TNA]

UDNEY, MARY, in Grenada, probate, 1808, PCC. [TNA]

UDNEY. ROBERT, in Grenada, probate, 1802, PCC. [TNA]

URE, JAMES MASTERTON, son of James Ure and his wife Margaret Innes, died in Grenada on 20 September 1827. [St Cuthbert's gravestone, Edinburgh]

URQUHART, JAMES, born 1729, a labourer from Aberdeenshire, a Jacobite prisoner banished to the Leeward Islands, liberated by the French and landed on Martinique in 1747. [TNA.SP36.102][P.3.382]

URQUHART, JAMES, born 18 August 1794, son of Reverend Thomas Urquhart and his wife Marjory Clunes in Rosskeen, Ross-shire, died in St George, Grenada, on 8 April 1823. [EEC.17483][F.7.68][DPCA.1095]

URQUHART, JOHN, son of Captain James Urquhart of Cromarty, died in Carriacou near Grenada on 9 September 1785. [AJ.1976]

URQUHART, JOHN CLUNES, born 17 January 1784 in Rosskeen, Ross-shire, son of Reverend Thomas Urquhart and his wife Johanna Clunes, emigrated to Dominica. [F.7.68]

URQUHART, JOHN MATTHESON, died in Tobago on 9 April 1853. [EEC.22440]

URQUHART, THOMAS, born 1751, emigrated via Plymouth aboard the Earl of Errol bound for the Grenades in March 1776. [TNA.T47.9/11]

URQUHART, WILLIAM, of Meldrum, Aberdeenshire, a planter in Carriacou in 1775. [PSAS.114.482]

URQUHART, WILLIAM, born 1758, son of James Urquhart in Aberdeenshire, a surveyor in Carriacou in 1771, died 1790. [PSAS.114.519]

VALENCIA, MOSES, born 1758 in Curacao, settled in Charleston, South Carolina, naturalised there on 12 December 1820. [NARA.M1183/1]

VAN BEAUMONT, ADRIANUS, a Dutch Reformed Church pastor in Curacao in 1660s. [Ecclesiastical Records of New York, i.186] [SAA.ACA.379/224]

VAN BECKE, Dr BALTHASAR, factor for the Assiento in Curacao in 1684. [SPAWI.1684.1563]

VAN BEEK, NICHOLAAS, Governor of Curacao from 1701 to 1704. [NWIC.I.81; 200.70][SPAWI.1702-1703.1327]

VAN BELL, ..., factor for the Assiento in Curacao in 1684. [SPAWI.1684.1563]

VAN BEUNINGEN, JONATHAN, Governor of Curacao from 1715. [RAC]

VAN BOSVELDT, JACOB, Governor of Curacao from 1761 until his death in July 1762. [NWIC.14.38]

VAN COLLEN, JEREMIAS, Governor of Curacao from 1711 until his death in January 1715

VAN COLLEN, JUAN PEDRO, Commissioner of the Slave Trade and later Governor of Curacao in 1720s

VAN DER LINDE, JOHN, a merchant, died in Curacao on 4 January 1816. [GM.86.473]

VAN DERDY, ..., born 1746, a servant, , from London to Grenada aboard the Mary in February 1774. [TNA.T47.9-11]

THE PEOPLE OF THE WINDWARD ISLANDS, TRINIDAD AND TOBAGO, AND CURACAO, 1620-1860

VAN DER STERRE, DAVID, a physician in Curacao

VAN ERPECUM, JAN, Governor of Curacao from 1682 to 1685. [NWIC.832/347; 467/145][SPAWI.1683.1249]

VAN GORCUM, PIETER JANSZ., a soldier in the service of the Dutch West India Company in Curacao in the 1640s. [NNC.57]

VAN HEYNEIGEN, G., a witness to Gilbert Munro's denunciation in St Vincent on 15 October 1823. [St Vincent Archives]

VAN LIEBERGEN, NICOLAAS, Governor of Curacao from 1679 to 1682. [NWIC.467.145]

VAN SCHEGAN, JAN, the fiscal of Curacao around 1730

VAN TAARLINGH, FLORIS, a planter in Curacao in 1710

VAN WEESP, GIJSBERT CORNELISZOON, a soldier in Brazil in 1635, then in Curacao by 1638, finally an innkeeper at Rensslaurwyck, the New Netherlands by 1664. [GAA.NA.1303/124; NA.1349/42]

VEITCH, Lieutenant R. H., of the Royal Engineers, married Marian Lardner, only daughter of J. Lardner in Barbados, in Dominica on 29 July 1863. [GM.ns2/15.498]

VERHOF, ..., a Roman Catholic priest in Curacao in 1750s

VERKUYL, NICOLAAS, a Dutch Reformed Church minister in Curacao from 1679 until his death in 1713

VEYRIERR, MICHAEL NATHANIEL, in Dominica in 1771. [JCTP.1773.274]

VIALL, CHARLES, born 1755, a carpenter from Norwich, emigrated via London aboard the Friendship bound for the Grenades in April 1774. [TNA.T47.9-11]

VILLAR, Captain, master of Le Biguare at Martinique in 1702. [SPAWI.1702.195]

VINCENT, MARIE ELIZABETH, in St Vincent in 1777. [JCTP.84.69/100]

VIOLETS, ..., born 1744, a servant aboard the Le Soy Planter bound from London to Dominica in July 1774. [TNA.T9/11]

VITTEUS, FREDERICK, a preacher of the Dutch Reformed Church on Curacao from 1635 to 1638, died in Angola in 1641. [SAA.ACA.157.14]

VITTET, JEAN BAPTISTE, in St Vincent in 1777. [JCTP.84.117]

VOAUX, CAMPBELL, born 1744, a surgeon from London, emigrated via London aboard the Diana bound for Dominica in April 1774. [TNA.T47.9-11]

VOLCKRINGH, WILHELMUS, a Dutch Reformed Church pastor in Curacao in 1660s. [SAA.ACA.379/224]

WADDINGTON, JOHN, constable in St Andrew's, Dominica, 1847. [DC:27.2.1847]

WALCOT, JOHN RICHARD, of Black Bay Estate, married Aline Bell from Stockton on Tees, youngest daughter of Thomas Bell the President of Dominica, in Grenada on 15 December 1859. [GM.ns2/8.289]

WALKER, ALEXANDER, son of Livingstone Walker and his wife Mary Ballingall [1730-1808], a ship-builder in Grenada before 1810. [Dunino gravestone, Fife]

WALKER, JOHN, born 1822, son of Andrew Walker, a farmer in Keithhall, Aberdeenshire, a clerk in the service of McHugh and Company, died in St Lucia on 8 December 1845, 'within two weeks of arrival on the island.' [AJ.5116]

THE PEOPLE OF THE WINDWARD ISLANDS, TRINIDAD AND TOBAGO, AND CURACAO, 1620-1860

WALKER, W.P., a surgeon, son of David Walker a farmer in Upper Park, Aberdeenshire, died in Grenada on 27 October 1838. [AJ.30.1.1839]

WALKER, WILLIAM, later in Antigua, then in St Vincent, 1778. [NRS.CS16.1.173]; a trustee of Walter Brown in Exuma, the Bahamas, in 1801. [NRS.RD5.48.399]S

WALLACE, WILLIAM, a planter in Tobago in 1778. [NLS.ms8794]

WALLER, MARGARET, wife of Reverend Edmund Waller, daughter of Reverend John Findlator in St Vincent, died in Brookheath, Hampshire, on 4 May 1848. [GM.ns29.675]

WALLIN, JAMES, son of Joseph Wallin in Leicester, died in Tobago in 1811. [GM.81.679]

WALLIS, ROWLAND, constable in St Mark's, Trinidad in 1847. [DC.17.2.1847]

WARDROBE, JOHN, from Edinburgh, a physician in Dominica, will, 22 August 1811. [NRS.RD5.21.175], probate 1811, PCC. [TNA]

WARNER, ASHTON, born 1780, Chief Justice of Trinidad, died there on 4 September 1830. [GM.100.645]

WARNER, CHARLES JOHN, in St Vincent, probate, 1801, PCC. [TNA]; a marriage contract between Charles John Warner of Bequia, father of Elizabeth Warner, and Robert Paul of St Vincent, dated 17 October 1792, Court House, Kingstown, St Vincent.

WARNER, ELIZA JANE, second daughter of Henry Warner a barrister in Trinidad, married William Hanbury Hawley, Major of the 14th Regiment, in Port of Spain, Trinidad, on 10 March 1864. [GM.ns2.16.680]

WARNER, FREDERICK, third son of Ashton Warner the Chief Justice of Trinidad, married Jeanetta Maria, third daughter of Reverend William Gunthorpe in Antigua, in London on 20 June 1843. [GM.ns20.200]

WARNER, GEORGINA, daughter of Ashton Warner the Chief Justice of Trinidad, married Anthony Clogstoun the Marshal of Trinidad, there in 1840. [GM.ns14.650]

WARNER, HENRY, a barrister, second son of Ashton Warner the Chief Justice of Trinidad, died in Jamaica on 25 July 1843. [GM.ns20.446]

WARNER, ISABELLA JANE, eldest daughter of Charles W. Warner the Attorney General of Trinidad, married Robert Farquhar Shaw Stewart, son of Sir Michael S. Stewart of Ardgowan, Renfrewshire, in Port of Spain, Trinidad, on 10 February 1859. [GM.ns2/6.534]

WARNER, JOSEPH THOMAS, in Dominica, probate, 1806, PCC. [TNA]

WARNER, Mrs MILDRED, born 1751, widow of William Warner in Dominica, died in Eltham on 1 November 1833. [GM.103.476]

WARNER, Reverend RICHARD ALBERT, born 1817 in Tobago, youngest son of Ashton Warner the Chief Justice of Trinidad, died in Plymouth, Tobago, in December 1845. [GM.ns25.326]

WARRAND, JAMES, died in Dougaldston Estate, Grenada, on 15 September 1838. [AJ.4742]

WARREN, DAWSON STOCKLEY, a Captain of the 14th Regiment, married Barbara Mary Grant, youngest daughter of G. Colquhoun Grant the Treasurer of St Vincent, at Morne Fortune, St Lucia, on 24 February 1863. [GM.ns2/14.515]

WARREN, ROBERT, born 1727, a weaver, a Jacobite prisoner banished to the Leeward Islands, liberated by the French and landed on Martinique in 1747. [TNA.SP36.102][P.3.390]

WARWALL, M. A., a book-keeper in London, emigrated from London aboard the Le Soy Plant bound for Dominica in December 1773. [TNA.T47.9-11]

WATHERSTONE, ARCHIBALD, in Trinidad in 1821. [NRS.CS17.1.40.180]

WATLEY, CAROLINE, wife of Joseph Watley the Solicitor General of Tobago, died on Pepper Hill, Tobago, on 24 September 1844. [GM.ns23.222]

WATSON, Mrs DOROTHEA, died in Dominica on 16 November 1827. [GM.98.94]

WATSON, WILLIAM, in Tobago, an executor, 1810. [NRS.RD3.336.135]

WATT, ANTOINETTE LOUISE JOSEPHINE, eldest daughter of Henry David Watt, died in Roseau, Dominica, on 2 June 1860. [S.1597]

WATTS, CHARLES, a planter and ship-builder in Georgia, a Loyalist, from East Florida aboard the Robert and Dorothy to Dominica in 1785, a Loyalist Claim. [TNA.AO12.75.115]

WATT, JAMES, a merchant, son of James Watt a tobacconist in Glasgow, died in St Vincent in March 1801. [GC.1600]

WATT, JAMES, from Cairnie, Aberdeenshire, died on Montreuil Estate, Grenada, on 29 August 1863. [AJ.4.11.1863]

WATT, ..., daughter of Henry D. Watt, was born on Chiltern Estate, Dominica. On 10 July 1855. [EEC.322778]

WEALE, WILLIAM, in Dominica, probate, 1806, PCC. [TNA]

WEBSTER, ANDREW, born 1778, died 1822 in Grenada. [GM.ns92.478]

WEBSTER, A. F., born 1780, died in Grenada in 1823. [AJ.24.9.1823][GM.93.287][BM.14.626]

WEBSTER, BENJAMIN ROBERT, a clerk in St George, Grenada, witness to deeds in 1819. [NRS.RD5.159.216/157.493]

WEBSTER, Dr CHARLES, minister of Old St Paul's, Edinburgh, later chaplain to the troops in the West Indies, died in St Vincent in 1795. [JSC.89]

WEIR, JOHN, was granted land in St Andrew's parish, Dominica, in February 1768, [NRS.GD126/4]; Commissary General of Dominica, married Elizabeth Grove, daughter of Elizabeth Grove, in Ashgrove in 1776. [GM.46.578]

WELLS, J. J., warden of St John's parish, Dominica, 1847. [DC27.2.1847]

WETHERALL, JOSEPH, born 1784, a Major of the 1st Royal Regiment, died in Dominica on 7 August 1833. [St George church, Dominica]

WHITAKER, JOHN, constable in St Andrew's, Dominica, 1847. [DC:27.2.1847]

WHITELAW, JOHN, jr., son of John Whitelaw a perfumer in Glasgow, in St Vincent in 1800. [NRS.CS18.706.26]

WHITELAW and WILSON, merchants in St Vincent in 1799. [NRS.GD237.12.25]

WHITE, ARTHUR, former Colonial Secretary of Trinidad, died in Paris on 24 March 1856. [GM.ns45.548]

WHYTE, FRANCES, youngest daughter of Charles Whyte of the 60th Regiment, died in St Vincent on 17 May 1834. [AJ.4518]

WHYTE, JAMES SHAND, eldest son of Reverend Alexander Whyte in Fettercairn, Kincardineshire, died in Gouyave, Grenada, on 14 December 1859. [S.1436]

WHITE, Mrs, wife of Michael White in St Vincent, died in Brighton on 26 January 1802. [GM.72.185]

WHITE, Lieutenant Colonel of the 80th Regiment, married Miss Greig, only daughter of W. Greig, in St Vincent in 1810. [GM.80.383]

WHITEHOUSE, FANNY, youngest daughter of Edward Whitehouse of Walsworth, Surrey, in Grenada on 18 August 1792. [GM.62.766]

WHITEMAN, ANDREW, born 1760 in London, from Grenada, died 1813. [GM.83.85]

WHITEMAN, ELIZA, daughter of Andrew Whiteman in Grenada, married Richard Fall on 17 June 1820. [GM.90.636]

WHITFIELD, GEORGE, born 1774, a barrister in St Vincent, died 23 August 1819, at the Lodge, St Vincent. [St Vincent gravestone] [GM.89.472][EA.5835.279]

WHITMORE, ANDREW, born 1759, a clerk, from London to Grenada aboard the Mary in February 1774. [TNA.T47.9-11]

WHITTALL, JOHN, in St Vincent, married Ann Whittall, third daughter of Thomas Whittall, in Bailey Irvon, Radnor, in Builth, Brecon, on 15 September 1842. [GM.ns18.535]

WHITTALL, JOHN, of Canden Park, St Vincent, born 1813, late of Pontywall Hall, Brecon, South Wales, died 9 April 1858 . [St Vincent gravestone]

WIGHTMAN, CHARLES, a merchant in Tobago, son of Charles Wightman a merchant in Anstruther, Fife, in 1778. [NRS.CS16.1.174];

he married Elizabeth Cooper, daughter of Arthur Cooper in St Croix, in 1800. [GC.1356]; a planter in Tobago in 1805. [GA.T.ARD.13.1]

WILBY, Major, of the 90th Regiment, married Anne Paul, eldest daughter of Robert Paul, President of St Vincent, in St Vincent, on 3 February 1814. [GM.84.406]

WILDEN, JOHN, born 1750, a clerk from London, emigrated via London aboard the Industry bound for the Grenades in April 1774. [TNA.T47.9-11]

WILDRIK, RUDOLFUS, a Dutch Reformed Church minister in Curacao from 1758 until 1765, died there in 1794.

WILKIE, PATRICK, in St Vincent in 1776. [NLS.Acc.8793]

WILLEMS, [or WILLEMSDOCHTER], JANNETGEN, from Amsterdam aboard the Jacob bound for Brazil, settled briefly in Curacao before 1645. [SAA.NA.1291/193]

WILLIAMS, ELIZABETH, wife of Charles Williams, the Assistant Commissary General, died in St Lucia on 1 February 1845. [GM.ns25.446]

WILLIAMS, JOHN, born 1745, a clerk from Bristol, from Bristol aboard the Neptune bound for Grenada in January 1774. [TNA.T47.9-11]

WILLIAMS, Mrs MARY, born 1795, eldest daughter of Sir Stephen Shairp, widow of John Thomas Williams a Captain of the 2nd Regiment, died in Grenada on 14 March 1819. [GM.88.585]

WILLIAMS, SARAH, born 1732, with Sarah Williams, born 1756, from London, emigrated via Plymouth aboard the Rachel bound for Grenada in January 1774. [TNA.47.9-11]

WILLIAMS, SARAH, born 1721, widow of Samuel Williams in Grenada, died in Dundee on 14 September 1809. [GM.79.984] [SM.71.799]

WILLIAMS, WILLIAM HENRY, a clerk in St George, Grenada, witness to deeds in 1819. [NRS.RD5.159.216/157.493]

WILLIAMSON, JOHN, born 1730, a labourer, a Jacobite prisoner banished to the Leeward Islands, liberated by the French and landed on Martinique in 1747. [TNA.SP36.102][P.3.402]

WILLIAMSON, ROBERT, born 26 July 1806, in Banchory Devenick, son of Robert Williamson, a farmer, and his wife Elizabeth, died in Tobago in 1827. [Banchory Devenick gravestone]

WILLIAMSON, ..., daughter of Walter Williamson, was born at the Hermitage, Grenada, on 27 July 1824. [S.495.730]

WILMOT, THOMAS, youngest son of T Wilmot a builder in Bristol, died in Dominica on 1 November 1807. [GM.78.86]

WILSON, ALEXANDER, of Shieldhall, Grenada, in 1776. [NLS.Acc.8793.2]

WILSON, BARCLAY, Provost Marshal of Tobago, died there on 1 October 1831. [PA.117][S.15.1232]

WILSON, JAMES, in St Vincent in 1796. [NRS.GD237.12.25]; in 1800, [NRS.CS18.706.26]

WILSON, JAMES, head-master of St George's Grammar School and minister of St Andrew's, Grenada from1874 to 1876. [F.7.667]

WILSON, JEANNIE, born 1846, daughter of Alexander Milne in the Mains of Esslemont, died in St Joseph's, Trinidad, on 16 December 1874. [AJ.20.1.1875]

WILSON, JOHN, of Garden Estate, Trinidad, died there on 26 April 1833. [AJ.4458]

WILSON, SILIAS JANE, only child of Alexander Wilson in Redhill, Middlesex, married Edward Nicholls from St Vincent, in Barnwell on 20 May 1847. [GM.ns28.200]

WILSON, THOMAS, in Tobago in 1776. [NLS.Acc.8793.96]; probate, 1801, PCC. [TNA]

WILSON, THOMAS, son of Reverend Dr James Wilson in Falkirk, died in Grenada in 1805. [AJ.3012]

WILSON, WILLIAM, late of the Customs in Tobago, died there on 25 January 1831. [EEC.18648]

WILSON, WILLIAM, eldest son of Hugh Wilson an accountant of 12 Atholl Place, Edinburgh, died in St Vincent on 7 December 1848. [EEC.21766]

WINDSOR, LEONORA, eldest daughter of S. B. Windsor, the Solicitor General of St Vincent, married Archibald Bannatyne, in St Vincent in 1814. [GM.84.674]

WINFIELD, ..., a gentleman from London, emigrated via Portsmouth aboard the Grenville Bay bound for Grenada in December 1775. [TNA.T47.9/11]

WINGATE, Reverend JOHN, in St George, Grenada, died there in 1789. [GM.59.955]

WINKWORTH, WILLIAM SAMUEL, a surgeon, eldest son of Reverend William Winkworth in Southwark, died in Trinidad on 4 September 1817. [GM.87.629]

WINPENNY, R. C., second son of Reverend Richard Cooke Winpenny, in Market Weighton, Yorkshire, died in Carriacou on 3 January 1851. [GM.ns35.334]

WINSTONE, CHARLES, in Dominica, probate, 1803, PCC. [TNA]

WINTER, NATHANIEL, from Martinique, married Miss Pitcher, eldest daughter of Isaac Pitcher, in London on 1 November 1798. [GM.68.1150]

WISE, WILLIAM, gentleman in St George, Grenada, leased Grenville Vale plantation in St George, to William Junor of St Patrick's, Grenada, on 28 April 1789. [Caribbeana,3.223]

WOOD, EMILY FRANCES, third daughter of Lieutenant General Wood, Commanding Officer of the Windward and Leeward Islands, married Alfred Bury of the 69th Regiment, third son of the Earl of Charleville, in Barbados on 20 June 1854. [GM.ns42.384]

WOOD, FREDERICK JAMES, born 1819, son of Richard Wood in London, died in Tobago on 9 February 1851. [GM.ns35.334]

WOOD, THOMAS, born 1784, son of William Wood in Tetbury, Gloucestershire, died in Curacao on 13 October 1811. [GM.11.657]

WOOD, THOMAS, former Colonel of the South Carolina Rangers, Superintendent of Indian Affairs, died in St Vincent on 3 August 1825. [GM.95.382]

WOODBRIDGE, EDWARD HERBERT, eldest son of Edward Collins Woodbridge, died in Dominica on 2 February 1850. [GM.ns33.558]

WOODGARS, JURGEN, in Bonaire in 1741. [NAN.OAC.172/43]

WOODYEAR, MARY, wife of William Woodyear the Customs Controller at Fort Royal, died in Martinique on 13 December 1801. [GM.72.182]

WRIGHT, ISOBEL, spouse of James Henderson, in St Vincent in 1782. [NRS.CS17.1.1.78]

THE PEOPLE OF THE WINDWARD ISLANDS, TRINIDAD AND TOBAGO, AND CURACAO, 1620-1860

WRIGHT, JAMES, born 1807, son of George Wright a writer in Lockerbie, Dumfries-shire, died in Tobago on 14 May 1832. [Dryfesdale gravestone]

WRIGHT, JOHN, in Dominica, probate, 1811, PCC. [TNA]

WYATT, SOPHIA LOUISA, widow of James Wyatt in Martinique, probate, 1803, PCC. [TNA]

WYLLIE, THOMAS, seventh son of ....Wyllie of Warburton, Montrose, died in St Vincent, on 11 September 1842. [AJ.4948]

WYLLIE, Captain WILLIAM, son of ....Wyllie of Warburton, Montrose, died in Tobago, on 24 June 1833. [AJ.4469] [DPCA.6.9.1833]

WYLLIE, WILLIAM, a planter on Greenhill Estate, Tobago, in 1836. [TNA. T71.1572]

WYNNE, ROBERT, from St Vincent, died in Little Ealing, Middlesex, on 11 February 1795. [GM. 65.348]

WYNNE, THOMAS, a Councillor of Tobago, died in St Vincent on 11 September 1842. [GM.ns19.110]

YEATES, DOUGALD, born 1814, son of Henry Yeates and Margaret Campbell, an engineer, planter and government official in Tobago, died in 1884.

YORKE, Captain FREDERICK AUGUSTUS, died in Trinidad on 26 April 1817. [GM.87.568]

YOUNG, ALEXANDER, in Grenada, probate, 1793, PCC. [TNA]

YOUNG, DAVID, a planter in Grenada in 1776, [NLS.Acc.8793.1]; before 1783. [NRS.S/H]

YOUNG, FRANCIS, born 4 March 1848, son of Matthew Young a schoolmaster [1818-1873] and his wife Sarah Tebbett [1825-1874], died in Richmond, Tobago on 9 January 1871. [Straiton gravestone]

THE PEOPLE OF THE WINDWARD ISLANDS, TRINIDAD AND TOBAGO, AND CURACAO, 1620-1860

YOUNG, GEORGE, in St Vincent, probate, 1804, PCC. [TNA]

YOUNG, JOHN, a merchant, formerly in Tobago later in Glasgow, partner of John McNeil a merchant in Tobago, a deed, 1771. [NRS.RD2.224/2.646]

YOUNG, ROBERT, born 1742, a carpenter from Edinburgh, from London aboard the Greyhound bound for Dominica in December 1773. [TNA.T47.9-11]

YOUNG, ROBERT BOYD, in Tobago, graduated MD in Aberdeen on 18 May 1811. [AUL]

YOUNG, THOMAS, a tide-waiter in Bo'ness, West Lothian, guilty of assault, banished to the Plantations on 11 July 1771, transported aboard the St Vincent Planter, landed on St Vincent on 4 February 1772. [NRS.JC3.37; JC7.36.367; HCR.1.106; JC27.10.3] [SM.33.497]

YOUNG, Sir WILLIAM, born 1726, died in St Vincent on 8 April 1788. [GM.58.562]

YOUNG, Sir WILLIAM, born 1749, Governor of Tobago, died in Government House, Tobago, on 10 January 1815. [GM.85.373]

YOUNG, Major WILLIAM, a planter in Carriacou, a bond with William Mutter, former Governor of Cape Coast Castle in Africa, subscribed in Grenada on 28 August 1766, witnesses were William Donaldson and Joseph Bourda. [NRS.RD3.239/1.161]

THE PEOPLE OF THE WINDWARD ISLANDS, TRINIDAD AND TOBAGO, AND CURACAO, 1620-1860

ADDENDUM

Some other shipping links.

Levant Galley of Amsterdam, master 'Luycjk Bontecoo', bound from Amsterdam via Madeira bound for Curacao was wrecked near Aberdeen on 16 July 1708. [ACA.APB.2]

Robertina, a brig, master Captain Stewart, from Trinidad to Greenock in January 1846. [TS1.1.1846]

St Jan van Amsterdam, a privateer at Curacao in 1670. [PCCol.1670.901-906]

Robertina, a brig, Captain Stewart, from Trinidad to Greenock in 1846. [TS:1.1.1846],

Swallow of Dundee, master William Hill, from Dundee to Grenada in 1773 and 1774. [NRS.E504.11.8/9]

REFERENCES

DC = Dominican Colonist

CGCA = Curacao Gazette Colonial advertiser

HS = Hayluyt Society

JSC = A Jacobite Stronghold of the Church, Edinburgh, 1824

JCTP = Journal of the Committee for Trade and Plantations

KCA = Officers and Graduates of King's College, Aberdeen

MCA = Marischal College, Aberdeen

NLS = National Library of Scotland

NNC = New Netherlands Connections, Chapel Hill, 2014

NRS = National Records of Scotland, Edinburgh

THE PEOPLE OF THE WINDWARD ISLANDS, TRINIDAD AND TOBAGO, AND CURACAO, 1620-1860

PCC = Prerogative Court of Canterbury

PSG = Port of Spain Gazette

RAC = Riches from Atlantic Commerce, [Leiden, 2003]

RGNA   Royal Gazette & Newfoundland Advertiser

SVW = St Vincent Witness

TNA   The National Archives, Kew

TS   Trinidad Standard

UAL = University of Aberdeen Library

www.ingramcontent.com/pod-product-compliance
Lightning Source LLC
Chambersburg PA
CBHW061737270326
41928CB00011B/2268